THEOPOETICA

Michael Witcoff
Copyright © 2020 Michael Witcoff

ISBN: 9798680451120

Acknowledgements

This book was made possible by those who came before me. Without them I'd never know what real poetry looks like, nor realize how far I am from their genius. I intend to submit an entry to the Western canon someday, and the greats of the past will be my guides.

I'd like to thank my editor, Michael Vlahos, for helping me to shape and clean up my rough draft. Having an objective, detached set of eyes is very useful for a writer and I'm grateful for his help.

I also owe a debt of gratitude to my various social media friends, specifically on Facebook and the *Brother Augustine* YouTube channel. I showed these groups of people two possible book covers and surveyed them for book formats as well. The responses to each poll were overwhelmingly in favor of one or the other option, which made my decisions very easy. Thank you to those who participated and helped me to provide you with the best book I can.

Last but not least, none of this would be possible without God. Without Him and what He's done for me I would still be miserable and depressed, a hollow shell in constant search of my next dopamine rush. I still get that way sometimes, as you'll read about soon, but now I have the insight to realize when I've fallen…and the tools and grace by which to restore my soul to sanity.

Foreword

Never once in my life did I plan on writing poetry. I didn't read it in high school, didn't care for it in college, and never gave the subject another thought until I was 32 years old. For about a year before that I'd been studying the art of fiction - storytelling, characters, dialogue, etc. I read more than a handful of books on the subject until finally finding John Gardner.

On top of writing with a skill unmatched in modern English, Gardner was a prolific teacher who gave workshops around the country. He turned the knowledge he gained into a series of books, in which he recommended the study of poetry. I had reached the point in my life where I knew that learning a new skill relied on submitting to a teacher. He mentioned <u>A Poet's Handbook</u>, by Judson Jerome, and so I found myself ordering a copy.

When the book arrived and I flipped through its pages, I was shocked. I had been expecting the kind of flowery sensitivity I'd always associated with poetry, but what I saw looked more like a technical manual. I never knew poetry could be an academic subject, and the way Jerome broke it down caught my interest immediately... and held it for all of a week. I quickly decided it was too difficult to tackle, and put it down in lieu of more books on prose.

A year later, as part of that journey, I signed up for Trace Crawford's *Complete Creative Writing Class* on

Udemy. As part of my procrastination and fear of actually writing prose, I decided to take on the Poetry module first. For some reason, it *clicked*. I had a lot more fun than I'd expected playing with the different forms, and remembered the old Judson Jerome book. Once I was done with the course, I went back through that book...and *this* time, I understood it. I began to play around with different styles, on different topics, with different meters - and found myself enjoying it for both its creative and meditative value. I ended up with a decent selection of poems, some of which have now been published on the *Saints Edward Media* and *Society Of Classical Poets* websites.

Though I had just completed about half of a non-fiction book, I felt the urge to share all that I'd learned on my poetic journey. It's likely that the urge was just another of the many forms procrastination and fear can take. But hey - it produced the book you're now reading, so all's well that ends well...right?

I've decided to write this book in three major parts, though the first two are blended together. The first section is my poems, and the second is my commentary on them. Though originally my layout for <u>Theopoetica</u> was to include all the poems first as a block - then all the commentary second as its own - a survey of my social media followers revealed a preference for the comments on each poem to appear immediately after the piece. The third section is my thoughts on the craft in general, including a larger discussion on the state of Western art.

You may prefer to read the poems and interpret them for yourself, completely apart from what I believed I was doing. Perhaps you will agree with Dream Theater, a heavy metal band, that it's *"better to save the mystery than surrender to the secret."* If that's more your style - and you'd prefer not to know how I interpret the poems myself - then feel free to skip the commentary entirely. I have no qualms about the notion that some art is better left unexplained; worse yet, the powerful impact a piece might have can even be ruined by the artist. I hope that's not the case with my own work, but I can't really be the judge of your own interior experience.

But if you'd like to know my own thoughts and artistic process, then feel free to see what each one means to me. Perhaps you'd prefer some combination; reading them first, chewing them over, and only later deciding to see if we were on the same page. I've decided to include the comments mostly for readers who want to learn the art of poetry themselves. And by "the art of poetry" I mean real, structured, *classical* poetry. I do not mean the formless self-expression that most modern poetry has become. More on that later.

I've also decided to include it due to common problems with scansion, or the art of discerning a poem's meter and form. Even trained classical poets can struggle to figure out a poem's meter, so if you read the poems out loud and can't figure out how they're meant to sound, I hope my notes can help you understand them. Most of these poems are being published here for the first time, but a few of them have been read (or heard) elsewhere. "The King," "Logos Rising" and "Freedom's Heavy Yoke" were published on the *Society Of Classical Poets* website. I read "The King" on my YouTube channel, *Brother Augustine*, as well.

In writing this book, I had several choices to make: which poems to include, in which order to include them, and whether to include my commentary on each one. Most books of poetry do not include commentary. Perhaps the poets couldn't be bothered, or perhaps they couldn't explain their decisions. Perhaps they wanted to maintain an air of mystery. So if you'd prefer to believe that I'm an enigmatic genius, ushering creative forces beyond my ability to comprehend, then please don't ruin the illusion by reading my comments.

Many poets have certainly chosen that route and built up an air of power and charisma around themselves...which they would lose were the "tricks" to be explained. However, this book is part of a bigger project for me; it is part of a ministry that also includes non-fiction, YouTube content, and - hopefully, with the help of your prayers - fiction and music as well. Each of those is itself part of a higher mission: to baptize the various forms of creative writing and re-instill a sense of Logos in Western art.

That being the case, I've decided to explain my creative process and choices regarding each of the included poems. I do this to demystify the craft so that perhaps you, dear reader, will pick up where I have left off. If I do my job correctly, and with God as my guide, then perhaps you will be inspired to do some writing of your own - and my hope is that, if you are one of those whom I'm trying to reach in this way, my explanation of the process will lead you into deeper study of both the craft and your own soul.

Most of these poems are of a spiritual nature. A few of them are not; they are poetic experiments, attempts to play around with form and perspective, or directly modeled after someone else's poetry. However, none of them include curse words, degradation, base behavior, or the glorification of sin. There is only one reference to sex in Theopoetica, and it's in the context of an old behavior I'm ashamed of and have repented for. I believe this is the absolute baseline for moral art: that even if it does not inspire the reader to higher thoughts, then at the very least it does not inspire them to lower ones. The key to writing in this way is to purify your own soul; entropic minds cannot produce beauty.

Lastly, I'd like to thank you for buying a copy of this book. I appreciate that you've spent hard-earned money on my work, and my goal as a creator is to pay you back with quality art. I hope that you enjoy at least a few of the following poems, and that they serve as a light in these dark and trying times.

In the name of the Father, and the Son, and the Holy Spirit.

Amen.

"The Man In My Mind"

There's a man in my mind and he looks just like me
(But he's perfect and loving and kind as can be)
So I look to the sky, on bended knee,
And wonder if I'll ever become him.

As I run my fingers across these beads,
Sending to Heaven my prayers and my pleas,
I doubt there's a cure for my kind of disease
But I'm trying to stay hopeful regardless.

God knows how I got this way - really, He does -
He's got records on file of how my childhood was.
I don't deserve mercy but He shares it because
He knows it wasn't always my fault.

I ask for the little things, like we all do;
For a job, for some comfort, for money, for food;
But the thing I need most is for Him to subdue
That dark demon deep in my heart.

And I know He can do it - He's done it before -
He's filled me with grace and made my spirit soar…
But then I forget and reopen the door
And the blackness comes crashing back down.

I suspect that I'll spend all the rest of my days
Rising and falling in different ways -
But no matter what happens, I'll always pray
To become that man in my mind.

Commentary On "The Man In My Mind"

"The Man In My Mind" expresses the vast chasm between who I am and who God wants me to be. We know from the Scriptures and Saints that earthly perfection is not possible - and yet, how few of us can stop from feeling rebuked at the slightest sin? Too often we look at ourselves, in our filth and our selfishness, and think that we can never be saved.

But God is merciful as well as just, and our desire to improve keeps Him with us. He knows our faults and why we have them. He knows what we chose and what we didn't. He judges us fairly; in fact, He is the *only* fair judge. The judgment of other people does not matter, because they can't see into our hearts. St. Paul takes this even further, writing in **1 Corinthians 4:3** that *"with me it is a very small thing that I should be judged by you, or by man's judgment. Yea, I judge not mine own self."*

St. Paul knows himself well enough to realize that he doesn't know himself at all - certainly not enough to be his own jury and judge. He further observes how far from perfection he is, writing in **1 Timothy 1:15** that *"This is a faithful saying and worthy of all acceptance: that Christ Jesus came into the world to save sinners, of whom I* *am chief."* Orthodox readers will know this verse well; we say it before we take Communion!

It is the struggle that we must engage in, regardless of whether the prize is achievable. You must get in the arena and fight the battle if you want to *"work out your salvation with fear and trembling."* **(Philippians 2:12).** Even if we can never truly reach our goal in the flesh, it's vitally important to have one; both so we have an ideal towards which to strive, and a reminder of our failings to keep us humble.

"The Man In My Mind" uses a combination of closed lines and enjambment (or "lines that don't actually end where they appear to end on the page") because I find that combination engaging. Too many closed lines and it looks too sterile; too much enjambment and there's not enough structure. The poem is written mostly in anapestic tetrameter, with the final line of each stanza being written in trimeter instead. There is also some metric variation within each line, but the base is anapestic.

"Posterity"

When your mind, so sharp and clear today

Gives way to age, that cage of atrophy

Should you desire endurance (not decay)

Your spirit lives on through your family.

For generations, all those you have shaped

And saved and prayed for, pulled out of the fire,

Will think of you and thank you for escape;

Your legacy will live when you've retired.

Or by proliferation of the flesh

A stamping of the image you contain

Two souls becoming one; divine enmeshed...

By these, immortal life you may obtain.

And God will look upon your life and smile:

"Well done, My faithful servant, through this trial."

Commentary On "Posterity"

I was a bit unsure about publishing "Posterity," fearing it could be perceived as more secular than intended. However, upon further reflection, I believe the poem can be justified as spiritual. Before I address that, allow me to explain why I wrote it.

As part of my study of poetry, I ordered a collection by William Shakespeare. It was the first book of poems I ever bought, and his skill with the written word needs no defense. But I noticed that in his earliest sonnets - each of which has the same theme, as I'll explain in a moment - there seemed to be something missing that I felt could make them fuller. At least the first ten sonnets in the book were all didactic in precisely the same way: they admonished the reader not to die without having children. For an example of what I mean, here is Shakespeare's "Sonnet Three:"

Look in thy glass, and tell the face thou viewest
Now is the time that face should form another;
Whose fresh repair if now thou should not renewest,
Thou dost beguile the world, unbless some mother.

For where is she so fair whose unear'd womb
Disdains the tillage of thy husbandry?
Or who is he so fond will be the tomb
Of his self-love, to stop posterity?

Thou art thy mother's glass, and she in thee
Calls back the lovely April of her prime:
So thou through windows of thine age shall see
Despite of wrinkles this thy golden time.

But if thou live, remember'd not to be,
Die single, and thine image dies with thee.

As you can tell, Shakespeare deeply believed that dying without children was selfish and a waste of one's DNA. But it struck me as I read his poems that one can raise *spiritual* children as well - in either case, helping to form a younger person. Not all are called to marriage or child-rearing, though I do believe all men should have both mentors and students. And so I decided to amend Shakespeare's message, adding that spiritual fatherhood is as worthy a task as raising a physical family. "Posterity" of course, is a Shakespearean sonnet.

"The Confessor"

Far from the bustle of city sounds

A tussle of two wills: the time and place

Which God set aside to make His display

Of the Truth to make known, and lies confound.

Baring its fangs like some hideous hound,

That old serpent, coiled, poised, ready to prey;

A snake always seeking to lead astray

So that God's faithful servants will be found.

First they took my fingers, so I could not write.

Then they took my tongue, so I could not talk.

Mangled and tortured, left looking odd,

Thrown from my home in the middle of night,

A sheep without sheepfold, leading the flock...

They took what they could; they could not take God.

"The Confessor" is a Petrarchan sonnet in (mostly) tetrameter, written from the perspective of St. Maximos. His life is a good reminder that our "friends" can often hurt us even more than our enemies can - and to always stick with what you know is right and True no matter what the consequences may be. Imagine how difficult it must have been for St. Maximos to go against so many of his peers and superiors. Imagine what he must have sacrificed by doing so. His status, his reputation, his promotion opportunities; all of that went away because he refused to cave into lies or to stop speaking the truth. He knew the price of integrity and must have been terrified to pay it. But with God's grace, and with God's help, St. Maximos was able to change the course of history by refusing to ever budge from the Truth.

Are there areas of your life in which you compromise for worldly rewards? For validation? Friendships? Relationships? Jobs? If so, your conscience likely feels pricked every time you've done it. That "small inner voice" is the voice of God, urging you to pick up your Cross and follow Him no matter where it leads and no matter what else falls apart when you do. There is nothing we can give up in this life which compares to what God has in store for us. St. Maximos knew it, and you probably know it too. The only question is whether you'll live up to your convictions.

"Freedom's Heavy Yoke"

It seems that man is most enslaved by freedom –
As when he's left unto his own devices,
The passions always over-rule the reason.

A mind weighed down by choices, badly beaten
Into submission by conflicting voices;
It seems that man is most enslaved by freedom.

And man will make his money via treason
When he runs out of patience for fair prizes;
His passions always over-rule his reason.

And faced with branching paths like back in Eden
He tends to pleasure, never sacrifices.
It seems that man is most enslaved by freedom.

Of wand'ring eyes and devil's impulse seeded,
A dose of dopamine, mind-fire ignited;
The passions always over-rule the reason.

Until help from Eternity is pleaded;
Divine assistance, finally invited;
It seems that man is most enslaved by freedom,
And passions always over-rule his reason.

Commentary On "Freedom's Heavy Yoke"

The theme of the poem is that freedom can be a burden when our will is not guided by God. Left to our own devices, we almost always make bad decisions regarding our diets, our relationships, etc. But when the Holy Spirit has freed us from our addictions, all of a sudden we can choose better options. We can choose health. We can choose life. We can choose love. We can choose God. That is why no external or political "freedom" means anything at all to the human soul; we must become free internally, as set free by God, before that word takes on real meaning.

"Freedom's Heavy Yoke" was the second poem I had published, both of which were submitted to *Saints Edward Media*. The first was "Tyrant," which you'll find later in this book. Part of my motivation for getting published was to get over my fear of criticism. <u>On The Masons And Their Lies</u> became a #1 Best-Seller in 4 different categories on Amazon, but that's a work of non-fiction and I did not feel vulnerable or exposed in writing it. Art is very different; not only is it much more difficult for me to actually create, but it shows my soul to the world in a way that non-fiction does not. I started studying poetry specifically to improve my prose, as recommended by Damon Knight and John Gardner. I never imagined, when I undertook that journey, that I'd end up truly loving the craft.

Whether my audience liked the poem or not was frankly irrelevant when I published it. The point was simply to write, polish, and publish - to show my work to the world. People seem to like it, which is always rewarding. "Freedom's Heavy Yoke" is a villanelle, a very specific type of poem with a very specific (and challenging) structure: There must be two "refrains" repeated throughout the poem, in very specific places. The best-known example of a villanelle is Dylan Thomas's excellent piece, "Do Not Go Gentle Into That Good Night."

Villanelles are not only fun (and especially time-consuming) to write, but to me they are like poetic weight-lifting. Even if you use the form rarely - or at all - the simple act of choosing a theme, picking two refrains, and filling out that "skeleton" with the rest of the structure forces the poet to choose every syllable incredibly carefully. I don't believe that everything must fit perfectly in every line, and in fact can find such perfection a bit boring. But the act of doing it - of poring over synonyms and rhyming words and stretching your mind and its creativity to their limits - helps open up new pathways in the brain that will aid you, I believe, in writing all other forms of poetry as well. A good villanelle is both an exercise in structure and a finished piece all at once.

"He Who Saw The Deep"

And when that giant, tyrant child
Took from men their proper due
They looked upon their wives, defiled
And knew not what they next ought do.

And so, in song, they raised a cry
Unified, though many strong
And prayed that Gilgamesh might die
Or recompense those he had wronged.

Inanna's wisdom, shaped with hands
From high above and heaven's might
Set, then, into motion plans
To make that wrathful king contrite.

O seeker of immortal life -
To be so humbled, by such strife!

Commentary On "He Who Saw The Deep"

I'm sure there are readers who were horrified at the sight of this. Especially if they had not actually read the Epic Of Gilgamesh, they may have mistaken the poem for some kind of approval of paganism. It most assuredly is not. It is, however, the first sonnet I ever wrote, as I experimented with the forms of Western poetry. I had just taken a class through HarvardX on *Masters Of Ancient World Literature*, and so Gilgamesh was fresh on my mind.

I first submitted this poem to the writing class mentioned in the Foreword, the *Complete Creative Writing Class* taught by Trace Crawford. It follows the basic outline of the epic, beginning with the people of Uruk crying out to their gods for help. Gilgamesh, a tyrant, had been sleeping with their spouses and otherwise acting like a bully. Through the guidance of Innana, Gilgamesh goes on a long quest; it ends with his learning temperance and good leadership. This message, though expressed through an ancient Sumerian tale, is both acceptable to Christians and as applicable as it ever was.

"He Who Saw The Deep" was supposed to be a Shakespearean sonnet, but it's written in tetrameter instead of pentameter. Truth be told, it took me several tries to write my first Shakespearean sonnet. But at least I made some pleasant-sounding mistakes along the way.

"He Is The One"

Who gave life for you, that you might give yours;
Who shed His red blood, to bathe you in white;
Who made Himself small, that you could be large;
Who emptied Himself, that you could be full;
Who baptized the world, as it baptized Him;
Who went to the grave, that you might ascend;
Who became nailed down, that you might be free;
Who fasted for days, that you might be fed;
Who took all that pain, that you could find peace:
A sacrificed Lamb, yet Shepherd of sheep.

Commentary On "He Is The One"

"He Is The One" is written in the style of St. Ephrem the Syrian. His poems would be considered Free Verse by classical Western standards, and have no discernible meter or rhyme scheme (at least not in their English translation). "He Is The One," however, is decasyllabic Blank Verse.

St. Ephrem's poetry is based on parallel, analogy, imagery, and symbolism. He often makes use of paradox in his poems, which is a large part of the Christian worldview. The highest King incarnates as a servant; He who cannot be contained was contained in the womb of St. Mary; *the meek shall inherit the Earth.* I think paradox is such a large part of the Christian life because it turns everything we're taught on its head: what the world tells you is good, Christ tells you is bad. What the world teaches to pursue, Christ teaches us leads to death. What the world rewards, Christ punishes. Our fallen world exists in a state of inversion, as do the souls of far too many who live in it. Black is white, violence is peace, sin is virtue, and so on.

Back when we used to have Christian leaders, this was not the case...at least, not to the degree that it is today. Orthodox Kings and Emperors punished vice and did not tolerate what God calls evil. The Byzantine Emperors did their best to align the Roman laws with the eternal laws of God. They expressed this desire in different ways, of course, but overall tried to steer their empires towards Christ.

The world we live in today does not even make a pretense of doing so; indeed, our current "Christian" President has a State Department that goes around the world forcing pro-sodomy laws onto Christian nations that do not want them. Mike Pompeo threatens them with sanctions for upholding the laws of God and brutally forces them to submit. Once these evil plans succeed, "Conservatives" like Charlie Kirk celebrate the "victory" and in doing so, side with Satan against Christ and His Church. Trump has done well on the abortion and child-trafficking fronts, and nobody can take those achievements away from him. But he's a very far cry from how a true man of God would dole out punishment and reward.

Since we live in an upside-down country, there have never been more opportunities to discern good from evil. In fact, it seems many people are turning to God - and realizing He exists in the first place - merely by observing the unmasked face of Satan in our culture. The worse things get, the more people put the pieces together; they realize that if strategic, coordinated evil is real - which is to say, that Satan is commanding a wicked spiritual army that manifests through corrupt and wicked people on Earth - then God must also be real. This recognition alone is often enough to begin stirring up peoples' hearts and minds.

Perhaps that's the greatest paradox of all: that the farther Satan advances his agenda, the more people turn to God. Not only is this paradox apparent around us, but perhaps it's God's way of making a cosmic joke: that the more evil things become, and the more evil people try to censor Truth and goodness, the more peoples' souls inherently realize that something is not right. They detach more and more from the insanity around them, seeking and finding nothing in the world that grants peace. Out of options, as a direct result of the wicked and their plans to enforce that exact scenario, people end up looking inwards and upwards instead. And there they find God, the same as He ever was, waiting with open arms to give what the world cannot.

"Contra Mundum"

The greatest pain a man can feel,
Or so the ancients say,
Is seeing clearly what is real
And yet, to hold no sway.

So keeping burning thoughts at bay,
And biting back his tongue,
A young man's soul starts to decay,
To leave the fight unwon.

And so, in hiding from the sun,
That man puts on a mask
While wishing he could cut and run;
To be himself at last.

Those above him, he's surpassed
In merit and in truth…
And all the wrath that he's amassed
He stops from coming through.

They say "obey" and "quiet, you…
Fit in with all that's fake."
To keep the peace, he doesn't spew
His anger at the snake.

Sometimes, to give himself a break
He takes that mask right off…
But quickly learns it's a mistake,

By their disdain and scoff.

So burning like a molotov
And ready to explode,
He plays the fool to back them off
And speaks in common code.

A time or two, he hits the road
To start a different scene.
He hopes to go from lead to gold;
Find others of his mien.

At first the new air feels so clean,
They treat him with respect...
But then the people start to scream
When he tells truth unchecked.

They want politically correct,
It turns out after all.
What once was fun, and free, direct
Becomes boorish and gall.

Persecuted like St. Paul
He always holds his ground,
Hiding from them - one and all -
Just how it wears him down.

And so he plays that awful clown
To clapping and delight,
Always smiling as he drowns

And choking back his spite.

Such pain it causes, being bright,
In this world of black;
It seems he's always in a fight,
Defending from attack.

And once he's gone he won't look back
At what he left behind;
His life must be a one-way track
To practice peace of mind.

But if you find yourself confined
Don't think that you've been cursed…
For He Who became Truth enshrined
Was hated most - and first.

Commentary On "Contra Mundum"

"Contra Mundum" means "against the world," and
that's exactly how I felt when I wrote it. I began this
poem during the coronavirus lockdown, in which
Americans were all but imprisoned without trial. The
poem begins with an overview of what the narrative is
about, and then "zooms in" to go more into detail.
Though it was written during a particularly bad time in
our nation's history, I also wanted it to cover many other
experiences that can be had even during better times.
The feeling of alienation, of starting over just to have to
start over again shortly thereafter, and of being alone
against everyone around you is one I'm intimately
familiar with. I am not always in that mood, of course,

but given the Orthodox "response" to the lockdown, lots of old feelings got drudged up.

Every single Orthodox bishop in America capitulated immediately to the oligarchs: they shut the Churches down, banned us from the Liturgy, and didn't put up a single ounce of fight. I felt abandoned, I felt betrayed, I felt angry, and I felt confused. Thankfully, I'm no longer in the state of mind I was in when I wrote "Contra Mundum." But it expresses what that week or two was like for me, and why I was so tempted to apostatize. I'm not sure whether any of our bishops realize how much they damaged the trust and faith of their parishioners through their complete non-response to these events. Protestant leaders are publicly proclaiming that the entire thing has been a hoax. They are suing various governments to re-open the churches, rightfully seeing the absurdity of strip clubs and bars being considered "essential" while the doors of the churches were shuttered. I am still awaiting a single peep from Orthodox "leaders," aside from Metropolitan Joseph's instruction that his priests are not to shut down services completely.

"Contra Mundum" is, by far, the poem that gave me the most trouble and the greatest challenge in this book. I wrote it in a four-line *terza rima*, or interlocking rhyme scheme. The style, which Dante invented for his "Divine Comedy," normally uses a three line structure with an "*a-b-a* / *b-c-b* / *d-c-d*" rhyme scheme. I changed it for "Contra Mundum" to "*a-b-a-b* / *b-c-b-c* / *c-d-c-d*" and so on.

"Contra Mundum" is written in iambic heptameter.

"Vade Retro Satana"

Speak to me not of disease or of death

Or of riots or looting or pain;

Each day brings me closer to my final breath

And scenes pass that I won't see again.

The friends that I've made and the things that I've built -

All these, alone, are my concern.

And my soul won't be weighed down by greed or by guilt

When to dust this old body returns.

And when that day comes and my parting word said,

There is nothing I wish to confess -

Except, as I lay there upon my last bed,

That to God and man, I gave my best.

So no, you won't drag me down into that hell.

I say no - drink the poison yourself!

Commentary On "Vade Retro Satana"

On the Medal of St. Benedict you'll find the initials for a Latin phrase: *"Vade retro Satana! Numquam suade mihi vana! Sunt mala quae libas. Ipse venena bibas!"*

Translated, the phrase means *"Begone Satan! Never tempt me with your vanities! What you offer me is evil. Drink the poison yourself!"* The phrase is both a reference to a specific incident in the life of St. Benedict and a spiritually sound principle in general.

I wrote this poem because I hate hearing about what's going on in our country, at least in the sense of the negative news (which is all our mainstream media reports on). Every story is about something horrible, over which neither I nor you have any control. Every hour of every day there is a new catastrophe, disaster, shooting, injustice, crime, or accusation. It never ends, because that is how the media makes money. It's a sad fact of reality that people tend to watch (and click on) negative items more than positive ones, so the media pays its bills by filling your mind with fear all day. Whether the stories are even true is generally irrelevant to their revenue.

When the "pandemic" began in early 2020, all I wanted to do was wake up, work out, go to my job, come home, and focus on God and my projects. It seemed that I was not going to be allowed to do this, since all anybody wanted to talk about was the coronavirus or the government response in some capacity or another. All day I wanted to tell people to stop talking to me about this because it was pointlessly ruining my mood and wasting my energy, but I had to be professional and sit there and nod and smile or engage them in the conversation. As I write this commentary, months after I wrote the original poem, things have gotten even worse in regards to what the average American desires to speak about. Now it's the virus plus the wildfires, plus the riots, and a whole host of other things that I am trying to best to ignore.

I decided to express that sentiment via Benedictine symbolism since I consider all these topics to be "poisonous" to the soul.

Though it's not possible to fully escape from the insanity, it's possible to withdraw into oneself deeply enough that it doesn't affect you quite as much. If one lives in the world, there is simply no escaping it. And since I'm not a monk, all I can do is try to end the conversations quickly.

"Vade Retro Satana" is a Shakespearean sonnet.

"The Master"

It's not her I hate; it's the character I play.

It's the jokes that he makes and the way she responds.

It's the calls he ignores and how that makes her fall harder.

It's the kindness he hides and the gestures he neglects.

It's the flowers he can't give and the songs he can't sing -

Because the second he does, she'll leave.

It's that flash of attraction when he says something cruel

Or cuts another man down in front of her.

It's the flirting with her friend that stings her poor soul

And the passion she shares with him after.

It's the text that she sends

Laying naked in his bed

And her boyfriend's response, full of trust.

It's the brain that he has to pretend not to have;

It's the caress he can't give;

It's the love he can't show.

Commentary On "The Master"

"The Master" describes my relationship with (and disdain for) what Rollo Tomassi calls "the burden of performance." He wrote in his article "Love Story" that, *"Men are expected to perform. To be successful, to get the girl, to live a good life, men must do. Whether it's riding wheelies down the street on your bicycle to get that cute girl's attention or to get a doctorate degree to ensure your personal success and future family's, Men must perform...The degree to which that performance meets or exceeds expectations is certainly subjective, and the ease with which you can perform is also an issue, but perform you must."*

More specifically, and in the context of this poem and the lifestyle that inspired it, my particular "burden" during my 20s was to act bad at all times. I was a lost young man with the wrong priorities in life, and I had to play a certain role to attract the kind of women I wanted at the time.

My experience with this burden, and the impact it had on me, goes well beyond the typical man's. Rather than seek relationships through utility and financial provision, I spent a decade of my life seeking fornication instead. It is a completely different paradigm in which the traits that make a man a good provider in one context actively preclude his attaining sexual adventure in the other. Thus, my burden was not to make and share money; it was to play a specific character which women chose for casual flings. Though I became that character more and more over time, I never lost the sense of "true self" which despised the fact that I was acting. This is why, among other reasons, I was intoxicated for nearly the entire extent of this period of my life.

Those neck-deep in sin are rarely sober as they drown; most have to snuff out that soft inner voice which tries to tell them they're doing something wrong. And though the human conscience can not be completely silenced, those who attempt it generally use alcohol and drugs to do so. A silenced or muffled conscience allows the actor to behave in a way which he or she normally couldn't. The inner alarms would be ringing too loudly.

The most painful part of this heavy burden was what happened when the mask slipped away. Even if I only "turned the character off" for a moment, I could see the attraction draining from a woman's face. If it happened over text, and she wasn't there in front of me, I rarely - if ever - heard from her again. I even recall one particular instance in which, after a couple months of "dating," I explained to a woman where I thought the country was heading and made a list of suggestions to help her survive it. I remember the quizzical look on her face and her saying "Oh, you're actually a good guy." She noted that I'd approached her with a different attitude than that, and the subtext was that I "should" have led with kindness.

What she didn't know, of course - what women rarely understand - is that if I'd led with kindness, we wouldn't have been dating at all.

To her credit, she actually seemed to appreciate that side of me, and we continued to see each other on and off for almost a year until she got into a serious relationship. Most women to whom I was accidentally kind simply dismissed me on the spot and went off in search of further maltreatment.

"The Master" is the most personal poem in this book and I wasn't sure whether to include it. I decided to as a cautionary tale to young men that, if they go down the secular route of how to attract many women, there's a good chance they'll lose themselves in the process. They'll get what they think they want, but they'll die inside as well. If you're one of said young men looking for "dating advice" online, looking up to the internet celebrities always surrounded by women, I encourage you to remember you can't inside those men's souls. You don't know what they sacrificed in order to get those "results." Do not mistake outer abundance for inner fulfillment, because a hollow man with "everything," in reality, has nothing.

The "he" in the poem is the character I developed; the "her" could be any of the women. It describes not my interaction with any particular woman, but my interaction with femininity in general (or at least with the fallen state of it). I will never fully recover from what I experienced in that world, but I know I've been forgiven by God. Eternal forgiveness does not mean, however, freedom from temporal consequences for our behavior. We must live with our choices and the results thereof, though in God's eyes our sins are wiped clean.

Dehumanizing as the experience was, I primarily blame myself. In my defense, I didn't know any better and was just doing what appeared to "work." But there are few experiences so jarring as watching women lose interest in response to kindness.

The title is ironic since "Mastery" of worldly endeavors is often barely-veiled slavery to the passions. Not only in the realm of seduction, of course, but in business and politics as well. We are told by countless self-help gurus that we must become "masters" of money or even of entire industries. We are lied to and manipulated by various marketers into believing that our lives will be worthless and pathetic if we do not spend all our time and money learning how to make more money and gain popularity. Our minds are filled with deliberately-triggered visions of how great our lives will be once we have what the world tells us is wonderful, and we're made to feel terrible by those same lying advertisers when they make us imagine our lives without their products.

The truth is that becoming more successful at sin - whether it's greed, fornication, or anything else - does not make you a master of anything. It just makes the Devil your master instead.

"The Master" is written in Free Verse.

"The King"

Lying lips win praise and fame,
And money, pow'r and wealth;
They grant great glory for your name
But cost the price of self.

For once a man betrays his plans
To be upright and true,
That blackening corruption finds
A crack to slither through.

And every further step he takes
Away from good and right
Is one less chance to stop the snake
Before day turns to night.

That pull of cash and fancy clothes
Has pushed him towards a fall,
And though he's got the world, he knows
That he's got nothing at all.

And so he sits upon his throne,
That king without a crown -
A god to minds of men alone
But to the saints, a clown.

Commentary On "The King"

"The King" was published on the *Society Of Classical Poets* website, and the response it got inspired me to include commentary in <u>Theopoetica</u>. People liked it overall, but a couple of the commenters - far more experienced with poetry than I am - didn't quite understand what I was doing with it. Whether that's a question of my failure to communicate clearly or their own struggle to understand various aspects of the poem, I realized that sometimes it can help the audience to have an explanation from the poet.

One of the commenters believed that this poem was about an actual Monarch and his struggles. He described how difficult it must be to lead a country in such a manner, and I'm sure it is quite difficult. Nonetheless, "The King" is an ironic title. It refers instead to what the world rewards and calls glory - the polar opposite of how Christianity works.

All over the internet you will find various men portrayed as "the king" of one platform or another: "the king of Instagram," "the king of YouTube" and the like. Without exception, such men are granted these titles on account of the wealth they've accumulated and/or the women surrounding them. For a secular man, women and wealth are the peak of masculine achievement. To be fair, it is not an easy task to accomplish what these men did. The problem is that it's worthless. Their need for validation and attempts to fill an "inner void" with the material do not lead to genuine fulfillment.

"The King" describes the descent of a man who is fundamentally good but is led astray by the traps of the world. I wanted the poem - as with all others - to be in line with Orthodox theology and anthropology. Therefore, we begin from a place of fundamental goodness and acknowledge that *"Temptation comes from our own desires, which entice us and drag us away. These desires give birth to sinful actions. And when sin is allowed to grow, it gives birth to death."* **(James 1:14-16)** The poem's final quatrain draws attention to a paradox: that what the world rewards means nothing in the Kingdom of God, and that the highest station Satan can offer is still below the feet of the lowest Christian.

Another criticism that I received after publication was that "structurally it's all over the place." That is not the case; "The King" is written in iambic heptameter. The lines themselves alternate between four feet and three feet, and this is consistent throughout the piece. The only variation in this poem is the line "that he's got nothing at all," which contains one extra syllable before the iamb "at all." One could also say that instead of three iambs, that line contains two iambs and one anapest.

If you decide to buy the Audiobook version of Theopoetica, you will hear me read the poem out loud - and, as with many of the others, that may help to clarify any questions about structure and meter.

Ideally, when a secular "king" realizes "that he's got nothing at all," he will stop looking to the world for fulfillment and turn his eyes to God instead. Then he will receive the only crown that truly matters.

"Cincinnatus"

Those who want to lead are rarely suited
To the task; they just aren't constituted
To withstand the tempest of temptation.
Men like them will ruin any nation.

The gold before their eyes is just too shiny -
Their power to resist is just too tiny -
And all their scruples seem to disappear
The moment young and nubile flesh appears.

Such men are drawn to power like a moth
Unto a flame; of crown or of the cloth,
It makes no difference to such men - they all
Forget that pride precedes an awful fall.

But there's a type of man who's fit to lead
And he won't make your state or nation bleed.
And you won't find him prancing on TV
Or dancing like a fool with some celebrity.

And you won't find him begging for your vote
Or promising a pauper your new coat.
And you won't find him practicing his speeches
Or reaching for your wallet as he preaches.

He's playing with his children in the yard
And teaching them about the sky and stars;
He's married to a woman soft and kind
And politics is farthest from his mind.

And so it goes, the cycle then repeats:
The qualified are rarely the elites.

Commentary On "Cincinnatus"

"Cincinnatus" is my observation that those who seek leadership are often unfit for the role, while those who are fit are largely uninterested in seeking it. In America it gets worse, of course, as one cannot win an election without becoming indebted - which is to say, enslaved - to various donors with no loyalty to the country, the candidate, or his base.

According to legend, Lucius Quintius Cincinnatus was a Roman dictator - for about two weeks - in 458 B.C. He was working the plow on his farm one day when, as the story goes, he was approached by Roman politicians who wanted to recall him to public service. He then put on his old toga, accepted the mantle of leadership, and led reinforcements to the Battle of Mt. Algidus - where the losing Roman Army turned the tide and won instead. Immediately afterward, he retired from public service and went back to his life on the farm.

He was made dictator again - this time, for three weeks - in 439 B.C. Again he dealt with the crisis and then shirked all titles and privilege, never holding the reigns of power for a day longer than necessary.

He did not cut deals with major corporations, he did not influence foreign policy on behalf of hostile nations, and he did not try to entrench himself or his family in permanent seats of power. He simply did his duty and went back to his wife and sons. These are the rarest of all men, it seems: those who accept leadership when the country needs them, but do not seek or desire it. Cincinnatus was a model of civic virtue, and was admired by George Washington himself.

"Cincinnatus" is written in heroic couplets, with variation in the opening stanza and certain other lines throughout the poem.

"Beast"

Rumbling down the driveway after work, my
Car nearly collides with a blurry shape;
Fur and teeth and those padded, stealthy feet
Make him as a phantom in the darkness.

That thing almost hit me - loud, awful beast!
That thing that wakes my pups when they're sleeping,
That rumbles the ground when I'm trying to hunt,
And always scares my precious meals away.

I slam the brakes and my body lurches
Forward, toward the beast; he's already gone.
Quietly cursing under my breath,
I cross myself and say "Lord have mercy!"

Hiding in shadow, safest in silence,
I crouch beneath the cover of bushes.
Ears flattened back and pupils narrowed down,
Muscles tensed and body taut and ready.

But now, senses heightened, body alert,
The primal side of man has awoken -
I ask myself, "were I not in this car,
Could I defeat this creature in combat?"

That metal monstrosity stands in place;

Thick smoke billows out of a hole in back.

My nostrils are filled with the scent; it stinks.

I hope my cubs are nowhere close to it.

I sit in my parking spot and decide:

Yes, I think I'll find out the answer now.

Unclick belt. Open door. Step outside. Roar!

I challenge the monster to show itself.

The hair on my back stands at attention.

I carefully search for the best angle.

My teeth could tear its throat with no effort.

I was born for this. I am a weapon.

My eyes lock on his, the battle begins.

We size each other up and each wonders:

"Why should I risk pain and death for this fight?"

And both of us think: "Because I live here."

Commentary On "Beast"

"Beast" is the only poem in this book which has nothing to do with God, apart from perhaps a meditation on the nature of cohabiting the Earth with the rest of creation. Instead, it's a blank-verse poem I included as an experiment in form and perspective. Though there isn't a rhyme scheme, each line has 10 syllables. It has the same basic structure as "Thief," in that sense, but with shifting alignment on the page to represent the perspective of its two characters.

It was inspired by the coyotes that live on my mountain. They bring me great joy, when they aren't too close to the house, and I love the sound of their pups all howling at once. Usually the neighborhood dogs get involved as well, and I close my eyes and smile at their haunting canine symphony.

I was driving home one night, close to midnight, when I pulled into my driveway. I saw a coyote staring back at me, eyes shining from the reflection of my headlights. It stood its ground and didn't budge until I honked my horn, at which point it dashed into the nearby woods. As I pulled my car into the parking spot and thought about the encounter, I realized it must feel that *I* was the one invading a home. As I opened the door and stepped out of my car, some spirit of battle possessed me and I found myself shouting into the dark. I challenged the coyote for dominance of the mountain - not knowing if it could even hear me - and simply asked it to come alone so the fight would be fair. He stayed in the woods, likely terrified of my strength.

Or perhaps he just doesn't speak English.

Either way the image stuck in my mind for several months until I found myself writing this book. I don't care much for the idea of "stylistic" poetry, in terms of manipulating the way words look on the paper. That seems to be more of a Japanese technique than a Western one, and they will often choose the paper type - and even its scent and color - as a larger part of their poetic expression. It's a type of poetry I make explore someday, but for now I prefer the Western expressions.

It seemed this encounter would make for a fun experiment...so I put the human perspective on one side, the coyote's on the other, and then centered the text for the shared and overlapping thoughts. I don't know if it worked; feel free to let me know.

"The Neutrals"

Oblivion is fate for those
Whose apathy outweighs truth;
Whose souls are but leaves, twirling
In the wind of pats on the back from the world.

The pariahs of Providence are
Lukewarm, spit out by all;
No master wants their service and
Their loyalty is worthless.

They trust not even in themselves -
But who can lay blame on those
With the knowledge to know
They have no strength?

Ignored by those who made a choice,
Whose roads lead up or down;
"Let us pass them by," say Poets
Who see their souls within.

"Of Neutrals we don't speak," they write,
"As they spoke not at all."

Commentary On "The Neutrals"

"The Neutrals" is based on Dante's "Divine Comedy." In that most excellent and sublime of poems, the "Neutrals" are a group of souls in the underworld who were neither hot nor cold; they simply *existed*.

They are the first group of souls (or "shades") that Dante encounters as Virgil leads him into the poem's Inferno. Dante writes, in the third Canto of the poem:

> *At once with certainty I understood*
> *This was that worthless crew*
> *Hateful alike to God and to His foes.*

> *These wretches, who never were alive,*
> *Were naked and beset*
> *By stinging flies and wasps*

> *That made their faces stream with blood,*
> *Which, mingled with their tears,*
> *Was gathered at their feet by loathsome worms.*

This is Dante's interpretation of **Revelation 3:15-19**, in which God says to the Laodiceans: *"I know your works, that you are neither cold nor hot. I could wish you were cold or hot. So then, because you are lukewarm, and neither cold nor hot, I will vomit you out of My mouth. Because you say, 'I am rich, have become wealthy, and have need of nothing'—and do not know that you are wretched, miserable, poor, blind, and naked—I counsel you to buy from Me gold refined in the fire,* *that you may be rich; and white garments, that you may be clothed, that the shame of your nakedness may not be revealed; and anoint your eyes with eye salve, that you may see. As many as I love, I rebuke and chasten. Therefore be zealous and repent."*

Holy Scripture tells us that being indifferent - being *neutral* - is a hateful thing to God. Perhaps this is because even those who hate Him must inwardly believe in Him enough to be angry; otherwise, Who would they be so upset about? I've often suggested that many atheists have a deeper belief in Christ than many nominal Christians do, as their entire philosophy is based on Him. It's a rejection of Him, sure, but at least they believe there's something - or Someone - to reject. Perhaps God will have more mercy on those who believed - but actively rejected Him for one reason or another - than on those who claimed to belong to Him but inwardly believed in nothing.

Extreme as that may sound, the Bible is clear that God would prefer for the Neutrals to at least be cold. In the end, I suppose only He can know why. It seems like one of many aspects of our faith beyond the capacity of human reason to comprehend.

"The Neutrals" is written in Free Verse.

"Tyrant"

For love of God and fellow man I grasp

A blinded tyrant trying to trap the wind;

A sign of hope, or faith to light the path

Is all I need to see the road ahead.

But then before the day is done, I fall

Right back into my old impassioned ways;

And yet despite the blackness of my soul

The Holy Spirit, given by God, stays.

I can't imagine why He does not leave

Just like the rest that I failed and let down;

And by that endless mercy I receive

I come to know why Jesus wears the crown.

He loves without end, though I go astray;

To show such love to others is the Way.

Commentary On "Tyrant"

"Tyrant" is the first poem I ever published, and I was paid $10 for my work. I could hardly believe anyone wanted to read it - much less actually pay me to do so. In retrospect it was probably not best for my progress to be paid for my very first poem; it set up a precedent that my work "deserved" money, despite how new I was to the craft. In either case I made more for my very first poem than I'll get for the sale of this whole book! I submitted "Tyrant" to *Saints Edward Media*, whose owner (Michael Sisco) graciously published it shortly thereafter.

He and I fought over the use of imagery for the poem, which I was completely against. I felt that poetry's imagery is what it evokes in a reader's mind, not a picture or something "concrete" to force down his or her mental throat. Michael retorted that without an image, the poem would get no views on the website.

I ended up compromising, which I rarely do, because I saw his point and, in the end, it's his website to edit. I was ultimately pleased with the image that I found, though I still believe poetry is better without pictures.

It simply describes how I feel, in a general sense: like an evil person grasping for something I'll never quite attain, since I can't even see the target clearly to begin with. I have a murky, semi-opaque notion of when I'm moving in the right or wrong direction; but inevitably, a short time later, God will reveal even deeper depths of my own evil to me, and I find myself starting at square one again. Sins I don't even notice one year strike my heart like a blade the next, and it seems this path gets harder the more devoted you are to it.

There's a saying I once heard: *"Don't wish it were easier; wish you were stronger."* I've applied that concept to my prayer life and, though it sometimes fills me with fear to do so, I continue to pray to see deeper into my soul with all the darkness and evil it contains. Then I am saved by God's grace from the depression that ought to cause, as He shows me that I am still loved and that perfection is not required.

My first spiritual father once put it like this: *"The closer you get to the Light, the more of your own darkness you'll see."* Sometimes I want to close my eyes, to delude myself that I'm good or somehow worthy of grace. But then my heart is filled with strength and I open them once more, glaring into the Inconceivable.

I'll end this commentary with one of my favorite quotes from one of my favorite Saints, Paisios the Athonite. He wrote: *"The more a person gets to know himself, the more the eyes of his soul will open and he will see his vast weakness all the more clearly. He becomes aware of his own wretchedness and ingratitude, as well as God's infinite nobility and compassion, and he is crushed internally; he is humbled exceedingly and he eventually comes to love the Lord even more."*

"Tyrant" is a Shakespearean sonnet.

"Thief"

And now I arrive at my darkest hour,
All hope abandoned and paradise lost,
As the baking rays beat down on my skin,
My lips parched like the desert before me.

And there is none to witness who I was
Or who I am; that I am here at all.
All I see are those stoic Roman guards,
Armor gleaming in the light of the sun.

No one will remember a sorry thief;
Another crumpled body beneath wood,
Untied and tossed into an early grave
With all the rest of the forgotten ghosts.

But O, what fresh hell marches toward me now?
The sweet silence of my final moment
Broken by a loud and rumbling parade -
The poor victim carries the cross Himself!

Followed by family and all of His friends,
Bearing witness to inglorious end -
Lord, thank you for sparing me such defeat!
Straining my lips, I smile with gratitude.

Bones crunch as they nail His hands and His feet,
Blood mingling with the tears of those watching.
He's raised from the ground as the cross goes up
And they stab Him in the side just for show.

I glance over and see a face full of
Resolve, as if He'd chosen this Himself.
I wonder what His life may have been like;
About what led Him here, to this moment.

A voice starts to speak, out loud, in my head,
And it says precious words: "God is with you."
And just when I think that I've lost my mind,
The voice says "Dismas, no - you think clearly."

But how can this be? What wizard is this?
Who, O Lord, can know the heart of man?
"As you have said, it is the Lord alone;
He dies beside you on this very day."

What tears I would shed, could my eyes make them!
What praise I would sing, could my throat make song!
But I of little strength cannot do more
Than to feel my heart filled with hope and love.

So I confess unto the nailed God:
"I stole some bread to feed my wife and son -
And yet I know that what I've done was wrong.
Remember me, O Lord, in Thy kingdom!"

The Man assures me I will see Him there,
Fully, more fully still than even now.
As my flesh dries out and rips like paper,
I suffocate under the weight of it.

But now this thief can die with heart at rest.

Commentary On "Thief"

"Thief" is a creative re-imagining of the final moments of St. Dismas, the Penitent Thief. In this version of the story, he is being crucified by himself, glad that at least there's no one around to see it. He feels bad for Jesus, Who he sees being followed to His death by all who know and love Him, until he realizes that Jesus is God. Confessing his sin and being reassured of salvation, St. Dismas dies at peace.

Few things bother me more than sitting quietly working on some project - or even listening to music, or doing nothing at all - when someone comes up to talk to me. It seems that when I wrote this poem, I transferred that feeling of irritation onto St. Dismas, getting creative with the original story in order to accommodate and incorporate it.

This one took me a little longer to write than most of the others. I had about 80% of it done on the first pass, shaping and editing the lines into proper meter as the ideas and imagery occurred to me. But there were a couple holes in the poem, or things out of place, that it took several more passes to really work out. I am very pleased with the result, and I like the general idea of turning Bible events into poetry. Judson Jerome holds the title for this feat, having written the excellent "Jonah & Job" back in 1991.

"The Thief" is Blank decasyllabic pentameter.

"Above The Sea"

Part 1

We're all bright eyes and bushy-tailed hearts
Electric with the pulsing light of life;
We laugh and drink and cheer before we start
Our mountain journey in the morning light.

Then the sun appears and we awake
To sounds of coyotes howling in the wind.
We pack up all our tents and leave our base,
Heading toward the steps where we'll begin.

We stake our claim in walls of rock and clay,
We scrape and climb upon our hands and knees;
Exhausted, bloody, hungry when the day
Then leaves us, blissful, laying in the breeze.

Tomorrow the ascent begins again;
We pray for victory and say, "Amen!"

Part 2

The second day begins and we arise -

Anticipation close, excitement near.

But then as we start marching toward the sky,

Facades begin to crumble; cracks appear.

My friend from back in college groans and falls

He says he's hungry and just can't go on.

By failing to prepare, he's hit a wall;

His courage has been sapped, his faith withdrawn.

The other climber watches, comes undone.

She cries and says she wants to go back home.

She tells me that she misses her young son;

She tries to fight, but in the end, succumbs.

If all else falls away, I climb alone;

Upward, onward, solid as a stone.

Part 3

Up here where all the air is crisp and clean,

A conquered mountain just below my boots,

I breathe in, smiling, feeling so serene,

And close my eyes with joy at hardship's fruits.

I think of friends who fell along the way,

Who all turned back in fear of the unknown,

And though I begged and pleaded with them, "stay!"

They all preferred the courtyard to the throne.

For glory only comes to those who fight;

And stories told of those who persevere

Fall short and miss the mark of shedding light

Unless the fighter learns to master fear.

And those who never try will never fall,

But neither will they ever live at all.

Commentary On "Above The Sea"

"Above The Sea" is based on my favorite painting, Caspar David Friedrich's "Wanderer Above The Sea Of Fog." I have the painting in my room, where I see it every day, and it resonates so strongly with me that I wanted to honor it with a poem.

I imagined that a group began the ascent with the main character, dropping off one by one due to various obstacles. The obstacles, as indicated by the "fear of the unknown" line in the third sonnet, are entirely psychological. They could have continued, but found excuses to quit. To me that seemed to make the protagonist's peak even more powerful, having not just outwitted the elements but outlasted other people as well.

Most people who wish to attain a goal will not do so. They will talk themselves out of it, give up too early, hurt themselves (or others) along the way, or end up losing their souls as they strive for glory.

The man who makes it up the mountain is "above the sea of fog;" he has conquered the distractions; ignored the noise; escaped the traps set for him and fallen into by others. There are countless interpretations of this painting available, and I'd like to explore them further in future poetry.

All three parts of "Above The Sea" are Shakespearean sonnets.

"The City"

I said to my friend, "today I leave town -
No, don't be sad, and please wipe off that frown,
For I made my decision long ago
But I've just worked up the courage to go."
His eyes went wide with disbelief, his hand
Gesturing 'round to the surrounding land.
His jaw dropped open and he asked me this:
"Does anything better than this exist?
The skyscrapers almost touching the sun,
Whatever you want - any kind of fun -
Ordering anything right on your phone,
Wireless energy harnessed and known?"
I put my hand on his shoulder and said
To my friend, "What you call living, I call dead;
I've seen what's on offer and I don't mind
Going somewhere else to see what I find."
I then took a deep breath and closed my eyes,
And did my very best to visualize.
I pictured my childhood, all that I'd seen,
And explained to him how my life had been...
As I walk through the halls of my first school,
I find myself surrounded by the fooled;
I slam the door and walk a different street,
But there's no difference in the fools I meet.
And so, escaping from the apes in crowds,
I try to find a mind amongst the clouds:
A thinker, lover, fighter all at once -
But everyone I meet's another dunce.

With woe and crushing pain inside, I then
Try living on a hill or in a den…
Because if what I seek is not out there,
Perhaps I'll find it praying in my lair.
And so I retreat, deep into myself
Trying my best to avoid all that hell.
Protecting my heart with thick fortress walls
Made of scrapes, bruises, and too many falls.
I close my eyes to think about the Word
A moment passes, and then I'm disturbed
By Facebook's beeping notification;
I swear, this thing just causes frustration.
I turn off my master and go outside,
Telling myself that at least I had tried
To escape from it; now I must make do.
I drive to the city, start walking through…
The reek of smoke, that makes me choke on wind
Polluted by chemicals, air that's been
Treated and poisoned by God-only-knows
What horrors I'm taking in through my nose.
Surrounded by stores that sell worthless things
And wives spending their husbands' cash on rings
And gossiping about women they hate;
It's enough to make me not want a mate.
And even if I did, who would I choose?
Their heads are all filled with that day's fake news,
Following famous people on TV…
Finding a good one is no guarantee.
Women beyond unworthy of the name,
Pink or purple hair, they're all just the same

Ugly shade of stay-away-from-me-please;
I've just got no interest in their disease.
Finding friends, no better! The men are worse!
Their lives and their hobbies are so perverse:
Man-children chasing cash (or the next notch)
Turning their backs on real culture, they watch
Heroes with powers and magic and capes,
Distracted from duty; they just escape
From a world whose weight they must - but can't - bear;
Instead, on their shoulders, they carry air.
No one to talk to about what matters -
I can't fake interest in brainless chatter -
And why work forty hours every week
Just to make it to a future so bleak
That the thought of it crushes me to dust;
Do I have any reason to adjust?
Fake fiat money printed and loaned out
At sky-high interest rates; there's no doubt
Goblins laugh all the way back to their caves -
Since we can't pay them back, we're all their slaves.
And they say "go to school, get a degree!"
But most students will never become free
From the grasp of their claws or wicked ways,
Stuck deep in debt for the rest of their days.
The Boomer will scowl, and sneer, and then say:
"I broke my back working hard at your age
To pull myself up and improve my life -
And I was in school when I met my wife!
But kids today, with your video games,
Smoking your weed and trying to place blame

On everyone but *you* for how things are;
I'm surprised you even made it *this* far!"
So the kids just get high and calculate:
There's no incentive to participate.
It all seems so hopeless, so pointless, so gross
That millions prefer to just overdose.
I'm snapped out of my nightmare by some scrap
That seems to be starting over some rap;
It looks like two gangs - and both black, at that -
Angry about the color of a hat.
One's wearing red, the other's wearing black;
For no other reason, they then attack
With such viciousness I can't believe it.
I'd call the cops…but decide to leave it.
I turn around and start to walk away
When another big group makes their display.
They aren't from around here, but still believe
They're entitled to break things and to thieve.
Babbling in gibberish I can't understand -
And when I try to help, they bite the hand
That feeds them with my taxes and my time.
There's no sense of gratitude; they just whine.
They always want more, and more, and still more.
Their want has no roof; their anger, no floor.
If I dare speak out against this Sodom,
Then they all just say that *I*'m the problem!
And my whole life will be ruined, ended,
By those who get paid to be offended…
By vampires draining our nation's blood;
By the kinds of people that caused the Flood.
Nobody speaks of poetry or God
And if you dare try they just think you're odd
Because they'd all rather speak of nothing -
Their conversation, empty and crushing -
Parroting the disaster of the day

Because they won't throw their TVs away.
Meaningless modern art foisted on fools
Either by those who don't know the right rules
Or created by conmen who must laugh
At the fact that people fall for their act.
So I turn from them all and go my way
Doing my best to survive one more day
In a world that isn't worth living in,
Filled to the brim with vice, evil, and sin;
Look where I may, no solution in sight -
Not one politician willing to fight.
They have money to make and position
To maintain, and limitless ambition
To sell all the (badly) ghost-written books
They can before people realize they're crooks.
And once that cat's been let out of the bag,
That each sweet word came with a steep price tag,
For a while people whine and they complain...
But then they forget, and just vote again.
Transhumanist devils hate creation
And leave, in their wake, pure devastation.
They try to build Babel, tear up the Earth-
All just to create the hell they prefer.
And they say "it's progress, forward-thinking -
Don't see the quicksand, ignore the sinking -
Disregard the medicated masses -
They just need a few more left-wing classes.
Then they'll see the truth, that all this is good -
A pod is better than a neighborhood -
That a spouse and children are outdated -
Dying alone's to be celebrated."
No reason to build what'll be torn down,
No reason to try and protect our town
When people who hate us decide its fate;
And once they're gone, it's already too late.

Why leave for descendants what they won't see?
Why do anything but take care of *me*?
Why try to make change and break through this wall?
Why bother doing anything at all?
Worse still, worst yet, on my desk, a picture:
A thin young woman holding the Scriptures.
She's wearing a sundress, a hat, and gloves
Gazing longingly at the man she loves
Who's staring right back, smiling ear-to-ear.
A young boy on his lap, love's souvenir,
Small hands wrapped around his father's strong arms
Knowing he's protected and safe from harm.
I long for that time that I've never seen,
Where kids play outside and the air is clean,
Where neighbors all love and trust each other,
And always look out for one another.
But then I snap back to reality,
To this grim cultural fatality,
To the atomized and isolated,
To the misery that's venerated,
To identity based in dysfunction,
To the rootless mass found at the junction
Of every nation, every sex and race
Mixed up, shaken, left to rot in this place -
And it just might work with God at the top,
But now He's one more item at the shop.
Briefly, my friend, here all are slaves to gold
And words, and smiles, and every thing is sold.
So now, you see, I say farewell; my train
Is leaving town. Through snow and sleet and rain,
Through thick and thin, wherever I may roam,
Through whatever waits along the way home.

Commentary On "The City"

"The City" is modeled after Juvenal's poem of the same name. He was one of the two most well-known satirists of his era - the other being Horace - and "The City" was his way of putting everything he hated into a long-form poem. Juvenalian satire is known for being venomous, whereas Horatian satire is more light-hearted and fun. Given the number of things I hate, I figured the form was appropriate.

Some of the couplets occurred to me at once, but most of them took time and effort to iron out. I made a long list of all the things that annoy me - both things I have to deal with in front of me and things I only have to hear about - and compiled them into what became the rough draft of this poem.

There was more I wanted to include, but which I was not quite able to fit in with everything else. Even worse, I wrote out a full page of what I thought was really powerful poetry...only to lose that page and everything on it. I cannot simply turn my creativity on at will; when it strikes, I write, and try to keep writing until the mood is over. I have no memory of what I actually wrote during that creative flood, because I enter into some kind of dreamlike trance state and am generally not directing the flow of words beyond making sure they stick to the meter and rhyme scheme I've chosen. I looked long and hard to find the missing page, but I was unable to do so. Perhaps some day, years in the future, someone will find it and have a good laugh.

Months after I'd begun work on this poem, I realized the whole thing could be an analogy for the City of Man vs. the City of God, or a transition from life to death; from the fallen world to the afterlife. I didn't think of that at the time I was writing it, but you're welcome to believe I did if that makes me sound smarter.

Ancient Christian poetry was derived from classic Latin works, and all of it is worth reading. If you have the time and desire to follow the golden thread, there are a couple of books I recommend in order. First I'd read The Latin Poets by Francis Godolphin, an amazing compilation of works from Catullus, Lucretius, Virgil, Horace, Propertius, Ovid, Seneca, Lucan, Juvenal, Martial, and others. Such works are the foundation of all Western poetry. The next step in the chain is the ancient Christian poets, who were well-versed in the writings of those authors. So second, I'd read Early Christian Latin Poets by Carolinne White. Men and women who grew up surrounded by the classics, either before converting to Christianity or simply as part of their classical pedagogy, wrote some incredibly powerful poems. My only complaint about the latter book is that no attempt is made to rhyme the translations from Latin into English, which makes it appear as if all the poems were originally written in Free Verse. They were not.

The italicized line near the end is taken directly from Juvenal's poem. "The City" is written in rhyming couplets.

"Solitude"

There is a sadness I sometimes feel
Deep in my soul, alone,
Surrounded by those who don't think
There's more to a man
Than what they see.

It happens in prayer, deep in thought
Lost in God
Perhaps when I'm writing a poem;
Down in the depths, in this fictive dream,
Time standing still all around me.

And then they walk up, interrupt, talk at me
And the beautiful spell is broken.
I'm dragged down from the clouds to the dirt
Clothed in time and space once again.

My heart sinks
To the bottom of wherever it goes
In those moments of stillness,
But raging -
So I grit my teeth and I smile and listen
Because they can't see the pain they've caused me.

I suppose I'll just save it for another day;
I'm supposed to be working, anyway.

Commentary On "Solitude"

"Solitude" was written at work - of course - shortly after another employee had interrupted me. I don't recall whether I was working on poetry, a short story, or taking notes for a novel at the time; all I recall is the surge of anger that arose in me at having to stop.

I sat there politely and professionally, listening to the other person complain about his day and his boss, inwardly praying the Jesus Prayer and looking at the icon I always kept on the desk. I gave minimum encouragement to the conversation, throwing out low-effort phrases like "interesting" or "sounds like it" to try and dissuade him from speaking to me further. However, some people simply do not pick up on social cues (and no judgment, since I didn't used to either). But my recognition that he was not capable of noticing my disinterest, rather than actively trying to ruin my creative and inspired mood, allowed some of the anger to simmer off as I tried to empathize with his having a hard day and dealing with a boss that wasn't treating him fairly.

The moment he left, this poem burst out of me. I wrote it in one pass; I don't think I even redid any words. By the time I got to the end I was in a better mood, and even snickered out loud at writing the final line.

Every creative person has a different preference. Some play loud club music; some write or paint outside.

But if there is any sound within the general vicinity of my hearing range, my ADD overwhelms me and there is nothing *beside* that sound I can pay attention to. As I'm finishing up this book's final edits, today, there is a truck somewhere in the distance that has been backing up more than I can understand - and every time it's in reverse, it beeps so loudly I can hear it. I had to put my earphones in and play relaxing piano music - which I'd also rather not hear, nice as it is - just to drown out the beeping. There is simply no other way for me to get things done, and once the "flow" is broken it could be hours or days before I'm able to enter back into it.

It can be useful to write every single day, for a predetermined period of time. Doing that consistently makes it easier to turn on the creative faucet at will, but even then it's nothing like an organic burst of inspiration. The key is to start writing the second that mood hits, and to continue writing the entire time it lasts.

"Solitude" is written in Free Verse.

"Morning Star"

Wise men have said darkness often shines bright,
And not all that glitters is made of true gold,
Because evil appears as an angel of light.

If you daydream of luxury, pleasure, delight
Then you just volunteer to be ruled and controlled.
Wise men have said darkness often shines bright.

When your guard is dropped down, you can't put up a fight -
In that moment you'll find that your soul has been sold;
Because evil appears as an angel of light.

The temptress will wait 'til your wife's out of sight
And you'll think she must love you because she's so bold...
Wise men have said darkness often shines bright.

If the joy of revenge makes you smile out of spite
Then you won't even realize your heart has grown cold
Because evil appears as an angel of light.

So then cover your eyes; God and soul will unite
And in doing so, break away death's evil hold.
Wise men have said darkness often shines bright
Because evil appears as an angel of light.

Commentary On "Morning Star"

The theme of the poem, that bad things can appear good, is taken directly from the Bible (as well as the life experience of anyone who's made this mistake). St. Paul writes in **2 Corinthians 11:12-15**, *"But what I do, I will also continue to do, that I may cut off the opportunity from those who desire an opportunity to be regarded just as we are in the things of which they boast. For such are false apostles, deceitful workers, transforming themselves into apostles of Christ. And no wonder! For Satan himself transforms into an angel of light. Therefore it is no great thing if his ministers also transform themselves into ministers of righteousness, whose end will be according to their works."*

That chapter is about false Apostles, those who claim to be righteous ministers of God but who secretly have an ulterior motive. They are the classic "wolves in sheep's clothing" that Christians are encouraged to avoid, and Paul exhorts the Church to be discerning about those who call themselves its leaders.

St. Cyprian of Carthage comments on this passage that Satan "invented heresies and schisms to undermine faith, pervert truth and break unity. Unable to keep us in the dark ways of former error, he draws us into a new maze of deceit. He snatches men away from the Church itself and, just when they think they have drawn near to the light and escaped the night of the world, he plunges them unawares into a new darkness...They call night day, death salvation, despair hope, perfidy faith, antichrist Christ, cunningly to frustrate truth by their lying show of truth."

St. Augustine added his own perspective on this verse, that "Satan transforms himself into an angel of light in order to test those who need testing or to deceive those who deserve deception. Nothing but the great mercy of God can save a man from mistaking bad demons for good angels and false friends for true ones."

So as with most of the Bible, this passage is written on multiple levels: the external level on which heretics and schismatics present themselves as Apostolic ministers in order to lead the faithful astray, and the internal level by which bad things appear good in order to test those faithful and discern the wheat from the chaff. In our daily lives, we are protected from the former by staying true to the canonical Orthodox Church; it is far harder to recognize temptation when it presents itself as desirable. In either case, the remedy is to stay true to Christ and His Church.

"Morning Star" is a villanelle in anapestic tetrameter.

"Logos Rising"

When Logos lived within the heart of man,
Then beauty bloomed and flowered forth at will -
And every house was built upon a plan;
Order's essence, captured and distilled.

Then Lucifer, in all his hate and pride
On gazing at the beauty of the saints -
To numb the pain and rage he felt inside,
Unleashed his darkness down without restraint.

He offered apples to his favored slaves,
The Darwins and the Newtons and the Humes;
They poisoned all the wells of holy grace,
And left mankind - by all our sin - consumed.

O Logos, rise and save the race of men;
O shine Your holy light on us again!

Commentary On "Logos Rising"

I wrote "Logos Rising" while reading a book, of the same name, by Dr. E. Michael Jones. You may have seen my interview with him regarding "The Conversion Of The Jews" on the *Brother Augustine* YouTube channel. It used to be on his YouTube channel as well, but has since been moved onto his BitChute instead. I did a follow-up video on my own channel afterward, addressing the conversation and some of the questions and criticisms I received.

Essentially, the poem details the erasure of Logos from the world we live in along with the hope that it / He will be restored and rise again. Of course He will at the end of time, but most Christians I know wouldn't mind if the world became more Christian and orderly in the here-and-now, too. Christ never promised it would… in fact, He promised the exact opposite…but the desire for things to become better is so deeply-rooted in the human soul that it's hard, if not impossible, for us to eradicate that desire completely and focus 100% of our energy and hope on the Second Coming. I personally struggle with the sentiment that "oh well, at least there's Heaven!" when it comes to inaction in the present world.

The book you're reading is part of my "action," as I've realized that the greatest act I can do is lead others to Christ. I can teach people to make money, I can write advertisements that sell their products, I can guide them in any number of worldly ways…but at the end of the day, none of that matters if their souls remain unregenerate and unsaved.

"Logos Rising" follows strict iambic pentameter and is a Shakespearean sonnet in every aspect (besides a couple near-rhymes instead of perfect ones). As poetic harmony exists when content matches form, it would be an awfully poor choice of me to write a poem about Logos in Free Verse.

I personally subscribe to the New Criticism theory of literature and I apply its tenets to poetry as well. The theory came about in response to various approaches to what gives a piece of writing its quality. Some said it was the intention of its author, others said it was the effect on the audience, and still others said it was the structure of the piece itself. New Criticism says that the quality of a piece depends on the harmony of its parts, of each aspect of the work enhancing and matching all the others. I believe this internal literary harmony fulfills the "structure" requirement and, on top of that, that the intentions of the author and the effect on the audience are a part of this harmony even though they exist "off the page." A piece should be internally consistent, with both authorial purpose and audience effect kept in mind. Everything should be intentional.

My highest hope for this book is that something within its pages helps you to turn from sin, pursue virtue, and "lay aside all earthly cares" to seek theosis with the Holy Trinity.

And some day, God willing, I'll even take my own advice.

Essay Introduction

I'm ending this book with a series of essays on the state of poetry as a whole. It will probably come as no surprise that my thoughts on modern poetry are not particularly complimentary; however, given that most poets of most eras tend to say similar things about the art of their time - and all tend to complain about the degradation of art in general - I am truly just one in a long line of people who have noticed and commented on such things.

What's different about 21st century American "poetry" is that, for the first time in world history, the internet has allowed us to see just how much bad poetry exists. I am tempted to believe that the craft has never been in such a sorry state - and this is probably true - but I cannot completely ignore the possibility that perhaps there was *always* a plethora of terrible art, from which the masses were protected by the lack of instant electronic communication. I imagine the truth lies somewhere in the middle.

Before I was banned from the poetry_critics subreddit, I spent a few weeks perusing peoples' work and offering my feedback where I thought it could be helpful. I tend to give fairly blunt, straightforward feedback - not just on poetry, but in all areas of life. This tends to be rather polarizing, and to separate my audience into two very distinct camps. The first - those who truly want to learn and improve - tend to appreciate it greatly and ask for further recommended books, courses, teachers, etc. They want to learn the skill and they're willing to do the work. The other group, composed of a far larger number of people, don't truly want to learn. They want to be *praised*. While there's nothing surprising about an artist who wants to be praised - and the aforementioned John Gardner would suggest it's every artist's real motivation - this second group tends to be composed of people who want to be praised just for the effort of trying, without regard for their level of talent or the execution of their artistic plans. They put something "out there" and ask for feedback, but viciously lash out at anyone who tells them their work isn't perfect the way it is. They appreciate only positive feedback, which massively stunts their growth. Perhaps they didn't have much potential in the first place - and many would-be poets really don't - but of those who do, a prideful and narcissistic attitude will stop their development in its tracks.

Most of the poems posted in that subreddit were bad. Exhaustingly, irritatingly, irredeemably bad. They were formless, meterless, rhymeless, and demonstrated absolutely zero knowledge or use of poetic technique. They write in a style I call *literary diarrhea*: spraying things on the page and then calling it "art." This is the most common writing style of the modern American "poet," who is angered by any suggestion that poetry requires technique. They just want to "express themselves" - which means writing about their feelings -

without regard for how the poem sounds or whether it will have a lasting impact. It is pure self-indulgence; rhetorical masturbation. To paraphrase John Gardner once again, a writer expresses him or herself automatically, subconsciously, by way of describing a unique and personal view of the world and by what words, images, and ideas a person chooses to emphasize or ignore. You do not have to try to "express yourself." You are always doing so. You are always communicating. Art which serves no higher purpose than for the "artist" to vent his or her emotions is not art.

Other Reddit "poets" did not have the basic grasp of English spelling, syntax, and grammar that is a prerequisite for writing well. Of those that know the language well enough to actually write in it, I found myself giving the same two or three pieces of advice over and over again.

By far the most common piece of advice I gave - and I generally only gave it to people I thought had potential - was that *your poem needs structure*. Oftentimes the poet would express an interesting idea and / or demonstrate a natural inclination towards the music of the written word, but was clearly not trained in how to structure that idea in a way that gave it real form, real boundaries, and real limits. Limits are important because substance is often derived from them; after all, how can one define a nation except by its borders? How could one know where one person ends and another begins, if not for the skin they live in and the space that naturally separates them?

Some untrained poets have a surprising predilection for rhyming, consonance, assonance, etc. With a little thought given to meter and syllabic consistency, they could (and hopefully will) become truly good poets.

However, I also believe that understanding meter and poetic technique is not the be-all end-all of poetry. All the technique in the world won't help if you can't process and communicate interesting ideas - and this brings me to the first major point of this essay. The reason that most poetry is bad - indeed, the reason that most TV shows, novels, and movies are bad as well - is not that the person lacks the capacity to learn proper technique. *It is that the creator thinks on a very low level.* It is the degradation of the mind and soul which have caused the degradation of art in general, as a person cannot communicate ideas higher than what he or she can process. It is not difficult to write about sex, eating, drinking, or going to work. These are basic, low-tier ideas that even the dumbest among us can understand. But there are higher grades of each of these ideas, going up in a scale in accordance with the development of the creator's spirit - as well as the ability to process higher-order thoughts and feelings - that can turn poems about everyday things into uncommon and thought-provoking art.

Even interesting poems, well-written with metrical and / or syllabic boundaries, are not the end of the scale. Though at one time I would have suggested that all the best poetry uses meter and rhyme, I now see those techniques as training wheels. You need to learn them if you want to ride the bike, but there is a level beyond it at which the training wheels come off. The freedom comes from having interiorized the training that uses crutches like extra wheels…and then riding off into the sunset without them. As I already mentioned, the overwhelming majority of modern American poetry is Free Verse and contains no technique. The "poet" skipped the race and tried to start at the end. The better way to do it - some might suggest the *only* way to do it - is to drill meter and rhyme and technique into your mind, to burn its impressions into the recesses of your soul - and *then* to write in either Free or Blank Verse. Then the technique will become a spice instead of the meal; then the very occasional and deliberate use of technique will make the trained and intelligent reader smile at its subtlety; *then you will only break rules that you understand.*

Everyone is familiar with Picasso's paintings…or at least, the ones he's most famous for. But did you know that before he made his first cubist piece, he had already mastered the style of realism? To really understand what I'm talking about, go do a quick Google search for "Picasso realism." You will likely not even believe it's the same artist whose pieces you've seen so many times before. And the reason is that Picasso used realism the way I'm suggesting you use rhythm and rhyme: *as rules that must be mastered before they can be broken.* Picasso's cubism contains no accidents; he knows *exactly* what he's doing, *exactly* why, and *exactly* where and how he's reacting against a past form of the craft. He is not just being weird for the sake of weirdness.

He is not just "expressing himself" or trying "to show his individuality." And yet, in his odd shapes, he does exactly that: he expresses his mastery of realism by breaking all its rules, and he shows his individuality by turning his training upside-down. But the point to remember is this: *He could never have done that if he hadn't mastered the basics first.* So too with poetry, you cannot simply jump to the end. You have to run the race first. And you have to crawl before you walk, then walk before you run. I've always believed that if you're going to learn a new skill, then it's worth spending the time and energy to do so properly. To that end I've always recommended the same book, the timeless classic Mastery by the excellent George Leonard.

But in order to truly grasp any of the above, one must first answer an all-important question: *How did things get this way?* My answer to that question, which will take up the remainder of this section, requires a couple of different approaches to understand. The first part is the *underdeveloped soul* of the average Westerner, and the second is the *conscious rejection of Western classicism* as a whole.

As I hope you'll understand by the end of these essays, these are intricately related problems. Interior and exterior are often related, though there is some nuance to understanding this dynamic that requires a proper explanation to unfold. Let's begin with the first part: the degradation of the soul.

__Tools Of The Trade And Inner Form__

Much has been written on the degradation of the Western soul and on the corresponding degradation of the exterior Western world. In the final analysis, inner and outer degradation are one and the same phenomenon, as it is not possible for the inner man to deviate from God without chaos being the outer result. However, the reverse is not necessarily true; it is far easier for outer chaos to remain at arm's length - beyond the point at which it can harm a Godly soul - as is attested by the countless Saints and martyrs who maintained their faith in prison or labor camps. Thus, it seems reasonable to suggest that outer degradation is the direct result, the direct effect, of inner degradation... but that we cannot conclusively state that the opposite is likewise true. *External problems do not always cause internal chaos, but internal chaos always causes external problems.* Subsequently, we cannot lay all the blame for the horrific state of modern art on circumstances outside of our own hearts and minds.

Therefore, rather than examining the outer world's "fall from grace," we will instead examine what has happened to the condition of the inner Western man and woman. The outer certainly plays a role in this, though again we cannot call it a direct cause. At most - and there is certainly something to be said here - we can blame the outer world insofar as the education system has gone from teaching *how to think* to teaching *what to think* instead. We no longer learn anything in school but how to be obedient corporate slaves; we don't even learn how to pay taxes and balance budgets unless we specifically seek out that information. In the ancient world students had to master many subjects - both the topic in and of itself, and how each related to the others. This is one of many reasons why, if you begin to study ancient writers, you will quickly discover that they were magnitudes smarter than the average American today.

We can also blame the media and public education - the two sharpest horns of the American Devil - insofar as people have become brainwashed to such an extent that it takes years of conscious un-learning just to arrive at the place from which all ancient students began; which is to say, a relatively blank slate that is capable of connecting cause and effect, rather than simply a sponge for propaganda. Of the small minority of people who realize they've been brainwashed and actively seek to undo it, very few will journey past the programmed emotional boundaries instilled in us since childhood in order to keep us away from alternate perspectives on certain important topics. School used to free the mind by feeding it the highest possible information and allowing it to build on what came before; now it simply builds a cage and punishes you for noticing the bars. But even with all this, in the midst of this insanity, people can think their way out of it and arrive at Truth.

I say all this to point out that the overwhelming majority of people in modern America are simply incapable of thinking on the level required to produce real art, and will not become capable of doing so. But I like to think that people who watch the *Brother Augustine* YouTube channel and read books like this one (or <u>On The Masons And Their Lies</u>) are amongst that tiny piece of the public pie that has both the capability and the drive to restore their souls to nobility. I do not write for "the masses." I write for *you.*

That being said, I believe you will be able to comprehend the following information, and to integrate it into the way you think and approach both art and your life in general.

Essentially, the quality of a piece of art begins with its reference point. That reference point depends both on the orientation of the artist and the heights to which his or her soul is capable of attaining. No telluric artist, for example, can produce works of a higher ideal; it is simply not in their nature, and beyond their capacity to fathom. Someone enslaved to the passions, in a state of conscious rejection of God, is not going to produce anything beautiful. Even if he or she has mastered the techniques of a given art form, the "inspiration from above" that is necessary for true beauty is simply lacking from their approach to the world. Their reference point is, to put it simply, too low. By "reference point" I essentially mean *the direction in which an artist is looking when he or she creates the art in question.*

Art can have one of three such reference points - from which it derives its meaning, its prosody, and its effect on the audience (or lack of any or all of these three things.) Let us begin with the lowest reference point, which is the base instincts and animal passions. This is the equivalent of an artist's "looking downward," and is constantly promoted in every modern American medium. It attracts the degraded and repels the whole.

In this category we find "art" focused entirely on the material, on the body, on its processes, on its wants and desires and fears and the necessity for it to replicate itself and hence "survive." Examples of this include "menstruation art," "art" depicting or describing sexual acts for no further purpose than to arouse the audience and awaken passion, and "art" describing states of intoxication and the methods by which it was induced. You will know a work of "art" is using the lowest reference point if you feel inspired to sin after looking at, reading, or listening to it. In this lowest category of "art" I put the work of, for example, Charles Bukowski and the majority of rap "music" - though both of these likewise contain a great deal of reference to the second possible point, which is the *self*.

In the case of referencing the self, consider this the artist's looking "inward." Have you ever noticed that almost every rap "song" is about the same topic? If you haven't, pay attention next time you have the misfortune of hearing one. You will realize that every "song," almost without exception, is about *the person performing*. It is about his or her goals, desires, sexual "achievements," or the amount of money he or she has attained or would like to attain. In such work you will find nothing befitting of a human being, at least not in the aspect which makes us higher than mere beasts.

There is nothing expressed which any pig, dog, or squirrel on this Earth would have trouble - could they speak our language - identifying with. All animals desire sex and resources, or "survival and replication" as some have called it. Such work serves mainly to glorify and amplify the pride of the performer and induce similar feelings in those who hear such things. As such, we can rightly call them satanic; they lead the soul away from God and place its focus on what is low. Needless to say, there are wealthy and powerful forces at play that pour all their demonic energy into the proliferation of such "art," either to sow the chaos that leads to more control or, in other cases, to encourage the very crimes that result in more money when the criminals get sent to for-profit prisons. The "artists" are, generally speaking, unwitting pawns in this game certain oligarchs play. They are offered money and fame and, having no higher reference point than themselves and their desires, sign their souls away without hesitation in exchange for these meaningless "rewards." Lord have mercy!

The third reference point - the only one which can produce true and lasting beauty - is God; or, at the very least, some other spirit or force which transcends the animal in man and places his attention on higher notions of love, self-control, spiritual development, etc. Artists with God as a reference point can be said to be looking "upwards," and those working in even otherwise-secular fields can often "baptize" these crafts through their dedication to a higher power. For example, heavy metal is often considered satanic. To be fair, some of it is.

But there are also bands like Theocracy, Stryper, War Of Ages, and Becoming The Archetype - bands whose music is specifically meant to glorify God. Even Black Sabbath had surprisingly wholesome lyrics from time to time. Thus you can see that what determines the quality of a given work of art is not even its genre, necessarily - there are even a couple Christian rappers - but rather, the reference point of the artist who is working within that genre or category.

Above self, self, and below self. These are the three basic reference points or "registers," if you will, in which and from which an artist can create. Mixed "registers" are also not only possible, but common. Art that glorifies nature, be it the love toward an animal or the beauty of a landscape, belong to the mid-high tier. Creation glorifies God. But a person whose soul is not open to God - whose nous is darkened, as the Orthodox say - is simply not going to be able to create from that level. The soul is asleep and the eyes are closed.

Having said all this, restoration of the soul to its proper place is the hardest of the main 3 problems with modern poetry to fix. They are: 1. Knowledge Of The Craft, 2. Grasp Of English, and 3. State Of Mind And Soul. Therefore, I will address it last - and we will begin with the first 2 problems that plague most modern artists.

1. Knowledge Of The Craft

The first of the 3 spheres which contribute to the beauty of a piece is simply knowledge of the craft itself. For an architect, this would entail the many fields of study which must work together to build a wonderful building. He must understand his materials, how they go together, which ones are incompatible, which type to use on which type of soil, how to protect the various materials from various kinds of bad weather or other dangers, how to prevent insects from taking root or destroying the wood, how to assemble the right team to bring his vision to life, etc. His craft is multifaceted and a lack of knowledge in any one area can bring the whole thing tumbling down.

A painter's craft involves canvas types and sizes, thickness of various brushes and their proper use in producing various effects, the ability to discern proportion and shade, and more. Someone with wonderful ideas, but a lack of painting knowledge, is not yet a painter; once he acquires all the necessary knowledge, he is able to execute his designs and produce the images he has seen in his mind.

Likewise, poetry requires the knowledge of certain tools. In fact, the very concept that *poetry is built with tools* is a revolutionary one to many modern "poets." They have been taught that poetry is just "self-expression;" that tools like meter and rhyme are "outdated" and "old-fashioned." The mere suggestion that *poetry has a structure* makes them recoil in horror.

However, the truth is that all great poets - even if they don't use all these tools, all the time - at the very least *understand* the tools and could use them all if they so choose. Good Free Verse poetry (poetry with neither meter nor rhyme) does exist in the world, and it can be powerful without classical form or structure...but as alluded to in the previous essay, every good Free Verse poet *learned the classical tools first* and then consciously chose not to use them - after having their rules burn deep grooves into the artist's mind. If you want to graduate to a higher level, you must learn the rudiments first. Once the tools have been learned, one is free to use or not use them as one sees fit, as works best with any particular piece. The difference is that modern "poets" use Free Verse *because they have to*, whereas real poets use Free Verse *when they choose to*. It is one of many tools in their arsenal - and they use it for specific reasons, within specific contexts.

For example, classical poetry makes occasional use of Free Verse. Can you guess what the reason is for that particular artistic choice? Can you guess what the poets hoped to communicate by the sudden breaking of meter, rhyme, and form? It was typically used in the form of plays, when the character speaking was overcome by emotion. By being written without structure, the lines themselves represented and intensified the overwhelmed emotions of the speaker; he or she was losing control, going outside of themselves, breaking their usual mode of being to express something at a high and chaotic pitch. Hence we see the use of Free Verse as a specific tool meant to communicate or sharpen a specific idea. "Self-expression" is the refuge of the untalented. It is not what Free Verse is for. One must learn the rules before breaking them, and then only break them with good reason.

Fortunately, this is by far the easiest of the 3 spheres to correct. Proper use of poetic technique is simply a matter of learning, practice, and feedback. You learn what the tools are and tinker around with them until you understand how they work. At that point, you know which ones to use in which situations, instead of trying to build a house with no blueprint. If you'd like to learn the basics of classical poetry, I recommend you begin with <u>How To Write Classical Poetry</u> by Evan Mantyk, and then graduate to <u>The Poet's Handbook</u> by Judson Jerome.

2. Grasp Of English

The second point of error, far harder to correct than the first, is simply an insufficient understanding of the English language. Causes for this error include being foreign-born and having to learn the language academically, having an IQ too low to understand the basic rules, or simply having never learned said rules due to various childhood circumstances. One can certainly be smart enough to learn English without having had the proper opportunity to do so, and such people have the best chance of becoming truly impactful poets compared to the other two (especially the second).

IQ is more or less fixed at birth, with a very small fluctuation becoming possible under various environmental circumstances. For example, a traumatic upbringing, early exposure to drugs or a poor diet, etc, can bring one's natural IQ down a few points. Alternately, a healthy childhood (physically and psychologically) in conjunction with a good education can bring it up a few points. Beyond that, you are more or less stuck with what you've got. People with a naturally low IQ will not be able to conceive of English on a high enough level to produce beautiful poetry, but they may have strengths in other areas that allow them to produce an excellent output in other fields such as, for example, singing or athletics. If you've made it this far into <u>Theopoetica</u>, your IQ is high enough to write poetry.

If you have the requisite IQ and simply lack a proper understanding of English, John Gardner recommended a book called <u>An American Rhetoric</u> by William Watt. It is a dense textbook, so I would only recommend you buy it if you are dedicated enough to make it through such academic exercises. Perfect grammar and syntax are also not strictly necessary in every single piece, though most attempts to break the rules come off as strange and unwarranted to me. Reactionary pieces against proper English - for example, writing in deliberately bad grammar - usually strike me as childish and likely only resonate with that group of people referred to by Harold Bloom as the "School Of Resentment."

3. State Of Mind And Soul

The 3rd and final sphere which affects artistic orientation is that of the soul or "interior" sphere. As the world outside requires order, so does the world within. There are countless forces at play both inside your own being and in the home, community, and nation around you. The directionless expansion and contraction of these forces leads to both inner and outer chaos, and hence one must impose a sense of order on these forces in order for them to interact constructively and not destructively. In the exterior world, the imposition of such order is the art and science of statecraft. That, however, is a topic for a different day.

For our purposes today we will focus on the interior world, on some of its inner forces and the proper hierarchy to which they should be subjected. Should this topic strike you at first as too esoteric - as irrelevant to a discussion of art - allow me to first explain why this is so important.

As I alluded to earlier, you cannot create something above your own level. If your mind is mush, you cannot produce beauty. If your soul is dark, you cannot produce light. If your interior form lacks structure, you cannot produce well-formed work. Thus, since the topic of this section is poetry - simply one aspect of a greater discussion on forms of art in general - then we must begin from the premise that *to create great art, you must first get your inner life in order*. The question then becomes what that particular order looks like, and the remainder of this essay answers that question.

Before I answer that, however, I'd like to address an inevitable objection to what I said a couple of sentences ago. By "great art" I do not mean art that is structurally sound or even impressive. Many such works have been created by profoundly unhealthy and miserable people, and this will be discussed throughout the remainder of the essay. Instead by "great art" I mean something that uplifts the soul and inspires it to greater heights. I propose that spiritually powerful and inspirational work can only be created by those in a spiritually inspired state. So what does that look like?

I'd like to offer you a 3-tiered paradigm which I believe will help you to understand the rest of the essay. I am not claiming that this specific hierarchy is immutable Truth, but rather that it's true enough to be a useful way of thinking. Therefore, I ask you to consider the proper hierarchy as being composed of *God, reason, and vitality.*

I'll define these terms in just a moment, but the bigger picture here is that when these are out of order within you - or worse, when one or more of them is missing entirely - then you will produce work which reflects that inner deficiency...not just in poetry, but in all other areas of life as well. I am of the belief that, as a general rule, the way we do *one* thing is the way we do *everything*. I think it's rare for someone to be intensely disciplined in one area and intensely lazy in another; disciplined people tend to be disciplined across the board, and the same is true for the lazy and their general lack of effort in life. Thus, to create true art, you must first make sure to develop and align your interior forces properly.

Let us start at the lowest force, which I am calling "vitality." This is the overall term I'll use to describe your bodily functions, survival and replication instincts, life experiences, sensory impressions, and how you feel about all of the above. It is the part of your being that you share with the animal world. As such, it belongs on the *bottom* of your inner hierarchy. If you allow this lowest aspect to guide or rule over the others, you will be living an upside-down life. Things will go poorly, you'll fail to see the connections between why they tend to do so, and you will probably repeat the same mistakes over and over again. A functioning inner logos, or sense of order and rationality, is necessary in order to live like more than a mere animal. *Vitality should be subject to reason.*

A poet without reason can write only of his or her lower, baser life experiences - and, needless to say, without form or structure. Some of the writing may even be interesting or thought-provoking. But unless that poet has a natural proclivity for rhyme and meter, then his or her "poems" are going to be poorly-written Free Verse. The mere study of classical art helps train and develop the reason, or logos, which is the next force on our list.

Reason is the logical, compartmentalizing, boundary-oriented part of your mind that, when developed properly, allows you to run your life in a sensible way.

For example, you may want to eat every piece of candy you see. Your life force and sensory memories make you desire to do so. But your reason tells you this is unhealthy, that it would have too much sugar, that it could lead to disease or even premature death. Thus, if your life is subject to your logos, you will make good decisions (at least more often than not) and there will be proper cause-and-effect reasoning behind those decisions.

As a general rule, other animals do not share reason with humanity - though some, like certain types of birds and monkeys, can recognize patterns and even make primitive tools. There is thus a spark of logos in certain higher (but still sub-human) life forms, but it is nothing like what a human being ought to possess and experience. Many, sadly, live with no rationality whatsoever; they drift from experience to experience like a leaf in the wind, blowing this way and that without reason or rhyme. Such people may lead interesting lives - indeed, I lived this way myself for longer than I care to admit - but their underdeveloped logos will never result in any sort of structured and classical art - much less a happy or healthy life! *Life without logos is rootless.*

A poet (or novelist, or painter, or musician) who subjects his or her life experiences to logos - to reason, to order, to form - will not only create more interesting art, having been granted by said reason to peer deeper into his or her own experiences and the meanings and lessons behind them - but that art will also have real, meaningful shape. It will not be random or chaotic...

unless that was a specific artistic choice. The poem will have meter. The song will be in a consistent key. The painting will have well-defined boundaries. All these are the result of a developed sense of reason, which ought to be trained throughout your entire life by approaching problems logically rather than emotionally and training yourself in classical art forms.

Collapsed inner form, or a lack of logos, is not just the primary problem with most art in today's America, but with most of the people here in general. Their lives are guided by social pressure and propaganda. Their "thoughts" are slogans they heard on TV. They have no boundaries which might discern where to go; no mechanism by which to reject that which is ugly and demonic. They are hypnotized in the truest sense of the word, made permanently suggestible by the deliberate destruction of their inner form.

Proper art is the product of a specific inner form, a structure which exists inside the artist. Technically speaking, bad art is also the product of an inner form (or lack thereof); we cannot create something exterior to us which is superior to our interior.

I use the term "reason" to mean (beyond just rationality) structure, form, conscious decisions about which tool to use, when, and why. It is the order and logic which gives a piece shape and form. It is the decision of which key a certain song should be in; whether it should be minor or major based on the song's overall theme and message; what tone the lyrics should take; whose perspective they should be written from. It is the choice of guitar tones, drum effects, vocal register and level of compression. All these things are consciously taken into account by artists and producers in order to give the most powerful and impactful shape to the seed or spark which will blossom into the full song.

With poetry, *reason* is the conscious selection (or at least, conscious recognition) of meter, rhyme scheme, level of vocabulary, choice of words, choice of imagery and sounds and which sensory effects to emphasize when - and in what order. These are the tools that give shape to one's self-expression, without which it is not poetry but simply a short diary entry. It is the answer the artist gives when asked about why a particular decision was made. The second part of this book is largely an insight into my own poetic logos, to demonstrate what I mean and - hopefully - inspire you to begin thinking about and writing quality poetry yourself.

At the top of the hierarchy, in general as well as ideally within ourselves, we find God. He is that Order above all Order, that Blueprint of creation, Who became flesh and was crucified and resurrected. With life and logos detached from God, you end up with well-structured work that does not uplift the soul. Perhaps it's a degenerate song that is technically pleasing to the ear, due to the harmony and rhythm. Yet its content cannot rise above the level of the creator - and unless that creator is subordinate to the Creator, the piece will lack the truly inspiring meaning that can only be produced by the Godly.

The most popular art forms in America - novels, movies, TV shows, and video games - are largely those which contain life and logos, but lack the final tier of the hierarchy. They are created and developed with the most expensive and advanced tools ever applied to these crafts. They have scientifically discerned what sorts of events should occur in these media - and even in which order - to maximize the emotional journey of the audience and inspire a desire to purchase the next game or watch the next episode in the series. These things are done with surgical precision, with a logos *par excellence*…but serve no higher purpose than escapism and distraction. The audience is viewed not as a group of souls to be nourished, but as resources to extract money from - and even potential addicts to create. Can you imagine what our country would look like if those same tools were applied to create Godly, edifying art?

Allow me to briefly pick on Bukoswki once again. He may have been a technically proficient poet, but his "poems" are bestial and low. I speak of the majority of his work, of course, as occasionally in poems like "Bluebird" he expressed something far deeper. But most are about intoxication and fornication and the nihilism of having nothing better to do. That's the output of someone with life and logos, but with nothing above or beyond *himself* as a reference point. Such people only have an abyss into which to gaze, an empty void that lacks all meaning and purpose, from which perspective none of their experiences have any grander design - and thus, their lives are pointless. The heart, mind, and soul are illuminated only by God; He swells the heart; He expands the mind; He fills the soul. Submission to Him results in an experience of life far vaster and more beautiful than can possibly be understood - much less experienced - by those without Him. Once you align your life properly to this hierarchy, your own inner form will take shape. Then your art will reflect this inner alignment, satisfying the audience on many levels as a result of the prosody of its parts.

In order to realign your life according to true hierarchy and order, you must subject your daily experiences to the use of reason. That reason, itself, must be subject to God and His laws. When all three pieces of this puzzle fit together, your life will be built on rock instead of sand…and the art you create will pay homage to your inner harmony.

But in order to do so, you must first deal with any *conscious rejection* that may still dwell within you. If there is residual resistance within your heart and mind, then you may run into artistic roadblocks that are hard to comprehend or work past. It's likely there's a lot of it still dwelling within you somewhere, and you may even have perceived an invisible inner wall which you can't seem to get past. If that's the case and you'd like to make a breakthrough, then simply read on to learn more.

Conscious Rejection

In addition to the artistic creation attempted by those whose souls are not refined, there is also the matter of *conscious rejection*. By this phrase I simply mean the active, knowing rejection of all that may potentially lead to the beautification of the heart, mind, and soul in the first place. I further say this specifically within the context of Western artists, as the impressions which activate their souls' latent resources will, often but not always, be different from those which work most powerfully on artists from other cultures.

If you're reading this book in the early 21st century, then you were raised among a generation which was taught to hate its past. If you are of European descent in particular, then you were taught not only that your country is evil in and of itself - but more specifically that your ancestors were evil as well. You were taught that the men who conquered the Earth, mapped out cities, charted the oceans, and introduced first-world living to humanity were actually a bunch of evil barbarians forcing their oppressive way of life on all the unfortunate natives whose paths they happened to cross. Certainly there was a degree of subjugation involved; I am of course not suggesting that European history was all puppies and rainbows. But the version of it you've been taught highlights and exaggerates the bad while completely neglecting the good.

Given that this book is not about modern culture wars, I will keep the current topic in its appropriate scope. I may later write about the bigger picture of all this, but for now I seek only to highlight the ways in which this particular form of warfare - which is psychological before all else - undermines the creation of what might otherwise be awe-inspiring music, architecture, poetry, and prose. The social engineers who control our nation despise beauty because it is based on Truth. Therefore, in their ceaseless warfare against the Truth, they must necessarily destroy any particular mode of thinking that might lead to the creation of beauty.

Their first attack against beauty was to deny its existence; millions (if not billions) of dollars have been poured into undermining the very concept that it exists. Advertisements with attractive people have been torn down. TV shows that display happy, healthy families don't get made. Doctors who tell morbidly obese patients to consider eating better and exercising are attacked for "fat-shaming," which is devilspeak for any behavior that might lead to the beautification of the body. Ugliness is exalted everywhere you look, and poetry has not escaped that wicked net.

Classical poetry is the product of a classical Western mind; the product of careful study, imitation, and improvement on Western innovations of the past. Every poet who achieved anything was comparing himself to those who came before him. He competed with the ghosts of giants, whose work he admired and sought to transcend. But then in the mid-20th century, a virus was injected into the minds of Western men and women. Rather than stand upon the pillars of the past, they were taught instead to actively despise them. Slowly, surely, over the course of generations, the inventors and innovators of the Western world came to be seen as evil incarnate. Our poets, our writers, our musicians, our playwrights - they've gone from being venerated as the heights of Western excellence to being denigrated as "a bunch of dead old white men." Nothing has been created as a result of this campaign that can hold the smallest candle to their work.

We are now taught that the forms of art they learned and practiced are "oppressive" with all their rules and structure. We are told that rules in general are somehow "products of white supremacy." In recent times even *objectivity itself* has been slandered in this way. The powers that be want you to lose your grip on reality - to detach your mind completely from God and His laws - and to dive into the hell of relativism that leads to drug use, promiscuity, and death. It is not difficult to find articles from mainstream "news" sources making the "argument" that even concern for one's own health is "fascism." Do you exercise? Watch your calorie intake? Desire to live in a strong and healthy body? If so, the Beast wants to harm you. It will, through its countless tentacles, try to convince you that being in shape is actually harmful to the people who aren't. It will tell you that a healthy family is "privilege," the subtext being that you must deprive yourself of this blessing out of a skewed sense of "fairness" towards others.

The nuclear family, as they are now openly stating, is "colonialism" and based on "systemic racism." There is no end to the buzzwords they create just to hurt you. Anything that might help you live a healthy and happy life is framed as evil and oppressive, whereas anything that degrades your mind and body is framed as "progress." Once you understand this, you can't un-see it. Every headline will make more sense and you will begin to comprehend the depth of their hatred for everything true, beautiful, and good.

It takes a critical, determined, Herculean effort to remove this virus and restore your mind to sanity. This awakening is not an overnight process; it requires careful and unbiased study of the facts, through first one set of data and then another, on topic after topic, slowly piecing the puzzle together until you finally come to the place that - in a serious society - you would have started at to begin with. But that is the situation in which we find ourselves: expending years of difficult and alienating effort just to arrive at the beginning. In the words of Nicolás Gómez Dávila, *"Today the individual must gradually reconstruct inside himself the civilized universe that is disappearing around him."* The more deeply you pursue this endeavor, the fewer people you'll be able to relate to on any or all of these topics. But you will have something that most people don't: eyes that see clearly and a mind that actually *works*.

Most people will not undertake this journey, even if they desire to do so. The social rejection, conflict with loved ones, loss of work opportunities, and other punishments - deliberately installed in our society - are enough to turn away all but the fiercest seekers. Are you fierce enough to do this? Do you have the courage to face scorn from all but the tiniest group of other free people? How far are you willing to go in examining your assumptions? Are you willing to take a scalpel to everything you hold dear - to everything you've been taught by those you've been conditioned to trust the most - and cut out the tumors where you find them, regardless of consequences? If so, you will be on a path that you have to walk mostly alone. You will also be among the few thinking citizens left in the country, and you will have won a prize that can never be taken from you.

I try not to judge those for whom this path requires too much; I understand the desire to just live a normal life. Becoming free in this manner often precludes people from living it, and many are pretending to believe what everyone else does in order to not be targeted by the wicked forces controlling our nation. So again - I understand the desire to simply not deal with it. But I must empathize with that desire from afar, as I cannot simultaneously participate in lies and go to sleep at night with a smile on my face.

This *conscious rejection*, as alluded to in previous essays, can be a valid creative choice in certain circumstances and with specific intent. Chosen intentionally, this would look something like the Amish *rumspringa*, in which a boy or girl raised in a strict Traditionalist society relaxes the "rules" for a period of time. Rumspringa ends with one of two choices: either the young Amish man or woman chooses to reject the Amish life, or they become baptized into the religion. The purpose of this is to test their faith and decide whether they would like to return to Tradition, after experiencing the opposite and making an informed decision. There is a return to form afterward, or not; it is a conscious rejection or acceptance. But that is not what has happened to society as a whole. It is now so deeply-ingrained into the fiber of our being that it has simply become the default position; it is the conscious *acceptance* of Western excellence that has become the wading into dangerous waters.

The problem here is two-fold. Firstly, it was not a choice made in a contained sort of way - to make a specific point and then return to baseline. Rather, it was the complete unrooting of society as we know it. There was never a return to form. Secondly, what many of these "rebels" thought of as their own free choices were, in fact, the result of suggestions made by intelligence agencies and their various organs such as the media and entertainment spheres. They are the victims of what can only be called *mass hypnosis*, by which their discernment of good or bad is first suspended or broken, and then anti-Western brainwashing was poured in by the truckload. The program seems to have worked better than its originators could have imagined: their victims began to victimize others in turn, completely of their own volition, without any further involvement from their handlers. The virus became self-propagating.

But a Western person consciously rejecting Western culture is like tearing the heart out of the body. It is removing the roots from which the tree springs. You live in a culture saturated with Western ideas, from the vehicle you drive to the language you speak. The most viciously anti-Western liberals in the country would be unable to express their hatred if not for Western technology. And even with the technology, they couldn't express such opinions unless they were protected by Western free speech. As is the case with so many modern groups, they owe everything they have to the system they hate. Hatred of one's culture is not a well-thought-out philosophical perspective; it is closer to a garment one puts on to be trendy. For those who seek status and acceptance by the group, that hideous cloak must look like a purple robe.

But now for the good news: what made your ancestors great still lives and breathes within you. It may be a small flame rather than a roaring fire, but somewhere deep within you is the same blood and spirit that ran through their veins. It is simply waiting to be activated by the impressions of the greats; those who actualized the Western potential and, subsequently, will resonate with and awaken the sleeping Western soul within you. We have their books to study and learn from; all you must do is reach out and grab what's being offered. You will never realize your potential while rejecting the power and achievements of those who came before you. Throwing your inheritance into the trash out of some misguided sense of "social justice" is to spit on the blood of your forefathers who fought, killed, and died for the culture in which you live.

Harold Bloom, for all his anti-Christian faults, did a tremendous job of collating the Western canon and articulating its defense. He spent his entire career at Yale choosing the best of the best, explaining what put those people and works into categories of their own, demonstrating how they built on and improved what came before them. I am not aware of any living professors who have achieved a small fraction of what Bloom did, and the mediocre minds paraded around as "intellectuals" are universally unworthy of your time.

The greats belonged to a previous age, but they left their legacies for you to find. They left their art, their poetry, their law, their prose. They left instruction on how they did what they did along with the reasoning behind each choice. The only question left is whether you will accept their offer. Will you elevate your soul into what it ought to be? Or will you get lost in the faceless mass of the rootless, directionless, nihilistic crowd? Only you can make that choice.

I pray that you will make the correct one.

In the name of the Father, and the Son, and the Holy Spirit.

Amen.

Made in the USA
Coppell, TX
07 August 2021

60133832R00059